Deep Purple
Slaves And Masters

Laura Shenton

"It's not the same band it was twenty years ago — how could it be?! The idea is to keep on broadening those horizons without losing the spark. New blood always helps that."

- Ian Paice, 1991

Deep Purple
SLAVES AND MASTERS

Laura Shenton

WYMER PUBLISHING
Bedford, England

First published in 2021 by Wymer Publishing
Bedford, England www.wymerpublishing.co.uk Tel: 01234 326691
Wymer Publishing is a trading name of Wymer (UK) Ltd

Copyright © 2021 Laura Shenton / Wymer Publishing. This edition published 2021.

Print edition (fully illustrated): **ISBN: 978-1-912782-83-3**

Edited by Jerry Bloom.

The Author hereby asserts her rights to be identified
as the author of this work in accordance with sections
77 to 78 of the Copyright, Designs & Patents Act 1988.

All rights reserved. No part of this publication may be
reproduced or transmitted in any form or by any means,
electronic or mechanical, including photocopying, or any
information storage and retrieval system, without written
permission from the publisher.

This publication is sold subject to the condition that it shall not,
by way of trade or otherwise, be lent, re-sold, hired out or
otherwise circulated without the publishers' prior consent in any
form of binding or cover other than that in which it is published
and without a similar condition including this condition
being imposed on the subsequent purchaser.

eBook formatting by Coinlea.
Printed and bound in Great Britain by
CMP, Dorset.

A catalogue record for this book is available from the British Library.

Typeset by Andy Bishop / 1016 Sarpsborg
Cover design by 1016 Sarpsborg.
Front cover Photo: © Marc Brans

Contents

Preface 7

Chapter One: *Why Slaves And Masters?* 9

Chapter Two: *The Making Of Slaves And Masters* ... 41

Chapter Three: *Touring* 67

Chapter Four: *The Legacy Lives On* 87

Appendices 105
   Personnel
   Track Listing
   Discography
   Tour Dates

Preface

I've been bursting to write this book for a while now! *Slaves And Masters* is one of those Deep Purple albums that some fans love to hate and for that reason alone, I feel strongly that this element of Deep Purple's long-standing legacy warrants extensive discussion.

How can a band loved by so many have been disregarded so exponentially by some fans on the basis of what was ultimately, a minor line-up change? Well, I suppose it depends on how you might choose to define "minor line-up change". It is certainly not my intention to try and change people's minds on their opinion of Deep Purple's 1990 album but equally, it is an important piece of work in their tenure and frankly, it matters. As you can probably tell, I think *Slaves And Masters* is a great album but I promise, I absolutely promise, to be objective in my exploration of the subject matter as I write about it.

This book is aimed at all of the Deep Purple fans out there, it is not merely a meandering on my own opinion — that would be a very futile and narrow lens through which to assess anything!

The purpose of this book is to represent what *Slaves And Masters* meant to Deep Purple as individuals and in terms of their legacy overall. In such regard, this isn't going to be the story of what *I* think the album sounds like, that would be boring — I'm merely the narrator here.

Many consider that *Slaves And Masters* had many things going against it. When I put my music historian's hat on, it seems very apparent that when the album was made, there was an initial enthusiasm within what was to become known as the MkV line-up. However, the fact is that there was always a question as to whether or not it was sustainable, especially in view of the fact that so many of the fans were all too unhappy with the absence of Ian Gillan as the band's frontman.

This book will examine those things in detail. I want to revisit the narrative surrounding *Slaves And Masters* because it is a relevant album in Deep Purple's discography.

As with any band, every member will have a different opinion on each of the albums they put out. As a result, I think it is tremendously important not to generalise. As someone who has no affiliation with Deep Purple or with any of their associates, in writing this book, I will be doing everything I can to quote good, reliable sources that will help to get the story of the *Slaves And Masters* album across with as much authenticity as possible. Due to this, you'll be seeing lots of quotes from vintage articles. I think they are important to document anyway because there will probably come a time when stuff like that gets harder to source.

This book is a gossip free zone. I want to present facts rather than all kinds of weird and wonderful speculations. Also, there will be nothing herein that is in the lexicon of "this song is in B minor so it probably means XYZ." Nope! Not happening! I want to present what Deep Purple experienced with *Slaves And Masters* and not what I did as one of millions of fans out there. This book is a culmination of extensive research that I intend to use objectively to offer a meaningful narrative on, what is ultimately a very worthwhile album in *Slaves And Masters*.

Chapter One
Why Slaves And Masters?

It is a commonly held belief that Deep Purple were one of the founders of hard rock in the early seventies. When *Deep Purple In Rock* exploded onto the scene in 1970 from the MkII line-up of Ian Gillan, Ritchie Blackmore, Roger Glover, Jon Lord and Ian Paice, few would deny that history was made that year in terms of that band making a statement; they were here, they were loud and they were very much in the public eye.

Throughout the seventies, a flow of particularly successful albums such as *Machine Head* (1972) and *Burn* (1974) established Deep Purple as an iconic band who made a significant contribution to rock music. By 1990 though, the playing field was immensely different, both within pop music and indeed rock. Most supergroups who were at the height of their success in the seventies were now harshly labelled as "dinosaurs". No matter what they put out in terms of new work, the likelihood of being susceptible to heavy criticism or even being ignored completely was an immensely high possibility. Of course, it would be flawed logic to say that "anything Deep Purple would have put out would have been met with a negative reception" but equally, the odds weren't commercially in the band's favour by this point in their tenure.

As *Kerrang!* brutally put it on their March 1991 cover to advertise a feature on Deep Purple, "Kan Old Kodgers Still Kut It?" (Urgh! So ineloquent but each to their own!). Further to this, in the opening page of the magazine, it was stated, "Old Kodger Special Part One — Is Ritchie Blackmore still the world's greatest guitarist? Or is he too old to give interviews? Tough talkin' Joe Lynn Turner steps into the breach and admits that Deep Purple's credibility has been lost."

But what about the hardcore fans though? Surely they were keen to support their favourite band into a new phase of their tenure? Well, yes and no. And that's where it gets interesting. Enter the recruitment of Joe Lynn Turner to form MkV Deep Purple in the absence of Ian Gillan as vocalist.

Many may remember *Slaves And Masters* as the album that heavily divided the opinion of Deep Purple fans at the time. 1984 had dealt the fans something monumental when the highly regarded MkII reformed and delivered on the generally well received album, *Perfect Strangers*. The reunion had been highly anticipated, especially after the occasional rumour of such reunion popping up in the music press at sporadic points throughout the late seventies and early eighties. For a good few years after MkIV Deep Purple with Tommy Bolin disbanded in 1976, a lot of people were yearning for their very much overdue Purple fix by 1984, when they finally got what they had been hoping for.

It wasn't to last though. After the success of the *Perfect Strangers* album and tour, things started to go astray come the time of making the follow up, *The House Of Blue Light*. Ian Gillan was fired in May 1989, not long after the release of the double live album, *Nobody's Perfect*. And to think that the remake of 'Hush' that features on the album had been released as a single to celebrate Deep Purple's twentieth anniversary that same year! As promised, this book is a gossip free zone and as such, it isn't my place to speculate on the whys and wherefores of Ian Gillan's exit from the band in 1988. Yes it happened, and yes it is a vital ingredient in the story of *Slaves And Masters*; it certainly isn't something that can be glossed over. In the same token though, I promise to remain neutral and whilst I will quote the band on what their experiences of the situation were, I'm not even going to attempt to analyse the rights and wrongs of it. People gonna be people and all that.

For what it's worth, as much as fans romanticise it, the reality is that band reunions seldom work out. Old rifts and tensions come to the fore again and conflicts are once again more occupying that the music itself.

In his autobiography, Colin Hart recalled the divide in personnel that was in place when it came to making *The House Of Blue Light*, despite the fact that *Perfect Strangers* had been a success; "The recording was slow and not unlike pulling teeth. The tension was palpable. Why? They'd just come off a record-breaking tour — they were by any standard in the rock business, staggeringly successful. Yet the demons were still there. It was as if Ritchie wanted out, but to what he did not know, so until he did, he would be obnoxious. Roger and Ian took themselves off to a quiet corner of the Playhouse to continue writing. Ritchie kept himself to himself and Paicey and Jon were, as ever, interested but non-confrontational observers. Me? I was bored! By the end of June, everyone went their separate ways, the record more or less finished, but not with any enthusiasm. This would not be a blockbuster."

Hart continued; "The camaraderie had just melted away, the five band chums had retired to their separate worlds keeping their own counsel and "phoning in" the show. The audiences didn't seem to notice and why would they? They get to see the band once every two years and, so high is the expectation, they forgive or indeed don't even notice a below par effort. I, on the other hand, saw the show every night and could compare the enthusiasm of the first shows of the tour to the "going through the motions" of the last. At times on the tour we had brought in recording facilities to tape parts of the show for inclusion in the next album which to me seemed a bit throwaway, but I understood it was done to complete a three album deal with the record company, Polydor... *Nobody's Perfect*, the resulting live album, was, according to Ian, the worst Purple album ever and he was ashamed to be associated with it. Easy, Ian! Well, I'd heard better for sure. I personally don't like live or even part live albums, but a lot do, yet the inclusion of 'Hush' was a puzzler, I'll admit, especially as it was done in the studios at Hook End Manor in Checkendon, England, as a jam in February of '88. Taking the piss, really. The arguments went on as to where it should be mixed, especially between Ian and Bruce (Payne — manager), the former plumping for New York, which naturally got my vote, as Roger, Ritchie and the management were based near there and, of course, me. The arguments carried on as to where to record future stuff. The thought of New York appalled Jon, however. A heated argument then took place fuelled in part by Ian's frustration with the way things were starting to fall apart and the fact that he was drinking quite heavily again."

Blackmore was quoted in *Burrn* in November 1990; "Two years ago I was getting fed up by Ian's behaviour, so he had to leave. I lost all respect for him. On stage, he sang beautifully, but it was different in the studio. We haven't been able to write any songs, so in the end also the others got fed up with him. But this topic is very invidious, because Ian isn't here to defend himself, so I don't want to go too deep into everything that happened, but I've also wanted to work with a vocalist that was able to sing a melody. In addition to that, we always had arguments with each other. His opinion about music is completely different than mine. At times it seemed to be purely out of principle — we could never agree on something. He also didn't like the distribution of royalties for authorship. When we reunited Deep Purple, we agreed on distributing the authorship on the band members that were really part of the songwriting process. The bulk of the music was just written by three members and not being divided to all five members, as it was done before... Ian didn't like it — besides, he had a problem with the manager. Right before he left, he strongly quarrelled with him.

In addition, he expressed a lot of unflattering situations in the studio. When we wanted to make some decisions, and told him that he was the only guy who wasn't supporting our decision, he just kept saying: 'Why should I agree?'... Even now, I can't say anything negative on his talent as a performer on stage, though I can't stand his behaviour behind the scenes. But he'll probably say the same thing about me. During gigs Ian was able to make cool jokes, but he always had big problems to improvise, because he loves it when concerts are monotonous. He didn't want to try something new, and sometimes it seemed to me that he was thinking: 'It's better to let things keep going like in the good old days...'."

Jon Lord was quoted in *Kerrang!* in March 1991; "I never really felt easy with Gillan's contempt for Ritchie, which showed sometimes. He was contemptuous of the man. I don't think he liked the thrust of Ritchie's material. He always thought he could do better but I've not seen evidence of that on too many occasions. I'm not going to be spiky about Ian because I think he's a highly talented man. He's number one in a field of one as far as I'm concerned. But I'm convinced Ian was pulling in a different direction, as started to be apparent during *The House Of Blue Light* and his desire to do this Garth Rockett tour. We wanted to get on with the album and he was off doing Garth Rockett... The first thing that came was Roger — funnily enough — saying 'Ian's not singing well at all, I can't get a performance out of him.' Gillan was being openly contemptuous of the material we were writing, saying 'that's bullshit!' then Ritchie made the comment — quite specifically — that he was not sure he wanted to carry on because he was having no fun. It didn't feel fun with Ian. He said 'If we're gonna continue, for Christ's sake we've got to enjoy it. It's the only motive anymore.' It was almost a relief to have it voiced. So the four of us sat down in a bar, called strangely, The Whip, in Vermont and said 'It's not working, is it?' And we all agreed with each other and decided we should do it."

All the talent in MkII Deep Purple was not enough to carry them onto making a studio album together after *The House Of Blue Light* and consequently, with Gillan out of the picture, there was a vocalist vacancy that needed to be filled. Colin Hart summed up how he saw the situation in his autobiography; "So, who would replace Ian in the spring of 1989? Would the fans accept Deep Purple without Ian Gillan? It was hard to imagine."

Before it was decided that Deep Purple would seek to recruit a replacement for Gillan, Blackmore had briefly been weighing up the prospect of reforming Rainbow, or perhaps even launching a solo blues band based project. There was however, good reason not to do this on the basis that he still had a good working rapport with Glover, Lord and Paice. Upon being asked why he hadn't released any solo albums and was continuing to opt to work within the setup of a band, Blackmore was quoted in *Burrn* in November 1990; "I'm very hesitant with these things. I know that people like Jeff Beck and Joe Satriani are releasing solo albums, but the question is: Will the people be interested in an instrumental album of myself? I'm not sure. In other words, if I don't feel good about it, I like hiding behind others. Well, maybe one day, when I drink enough of these (pointing to the German beer), I'll have the confidence to release one. Sometimes I feel like recording an album like that, and I might do it someday, but not now."

With Gillan out of the band, the remaining members of MkII were initially keen on bringing in Jimi Jamison of Survivor fame. It sounds like it would have been an exciting combination and in a number of interviews, the other members of Deep Purple seemed to have felt this way but disappointingly for them, Jamison was strongly discouraged by his management. Jon Lord was quoted in *Radio & Records* in November 1990; "One guy, Jimi Jamison from Survivor, was practically in the band — until his management decided that it would 'harm his solo career'.""

With Jamison out of the picture and back to focussing on other projects, a number of names came up. After still no luck in finding a singer, with some reluctance, the suggestion of Joe Lynn Turner was put forward. Jon Lord was quoted in *Keyboard* in January 1994; "One of us said 'Why not try it with Joe Lynn Turner?' And the others said, 'Not Joe again!' I mean, he once was in Rainbow, then wasn't and then was — he was a kind of a "rent-a-singer"! But Joe agreed with the audition, something which surprised me, and he came and he sang like an angel, wonderful!... To make a long story short: somewhere during these auditions we said to ourselves: since Gillan isn't the only one who can sing, there has to be someone else, so why not Joe?"

Glover was quoted of Turner's recruitment to Deep Purple in *Metal Hammer* in October 1990; "He wasn't the obvious choice for the band. I didn't even consider it and I didn't hear his name until quite late. We started listening to the usual mountain of tapes. About ninety five percent of the tapes were Robert Plant sound-alikes which is a helluva testament to Robert, but we weren't looking for that at all. We wanted someone with a deeper, thicker voice, not something high and whiney. We homed in on a couple of singers and started having auditions. We found some excellent singers and we'd settled on one guy but I won't say who because I don't want to embarrass him. But after a few days Ritchie said he wished he was more excited by the singer. You need a frontman and a character as well. This guy was a brilliant singer but it didn't gel. We wanted someone who would let us write but had strong ideas of his own. It was a very frustrating time. Then Joe's name came up, mentioned by Ritchie from his happy memories with Rainbow. He was in Rainbow when we split up to reform Purple in '84. Joe had joined in 1980 so he was with the band for four years. When his name came up, I went 'Absolutely no way.' I must add there is nothing personal in that. I felt the way people would view the Rainbow connection would be, horrible."

Jon Lord said in *Kerrang!* in March 1991; "Roger had a little trouble with Joe Lynn Turner, on a personal level, not so much on a singing level, when they were together in Rainbow. I have not enquired as to the nature of that. It may have been something as stupid as arguing over a woman. But they've sorted it out marvellously. They spent an enormous amount of time together working on the lyrics for this album and I think they've really bonded, formed a really good pact."

Joe Lynn Turner was quoted in the *Asbury Park Press* November 1990; "They already had somebody — a friend of mine, actually. And they thought he was gonna be the guy. But they were not as excited about this as they wanted to be. They were all just kind of mucking around. They got this great singer right? But they're going: 'How come we're not excited? How come we're not going through the roof about this?' So Ritchie, as a last-minute resort, just said, 'Why don't we get Joe up to have a sing?' Because, everybody in the beginning was going: 'Please. Deep Rainbow? Please, let's not even think of Joe Lynn Turner. Enough already.' And I knew that. I wasn't slighted. They're still my friends. So I went up to Vermont, where they were rehearsing under ungodly conditions. God knows why this band goes through that. Rats... dead rats. We were up in a golf club. The bar of a golf club. In the winter. There's no one there. It's desolate. It smells like beer, in the rug. So I went up there, four hours up from New York. I walked in. Ritchie immediately started playing 'Hey Joe', which we taped on a sixteen-track, later to be released. First off thing. And the chemistry started happening. The magic. Bam, bam. We started writing 'The Cut Runs Deep'. And everybody just started looking at each other. 'Well, this is what we've been looking for! A kick in the (pants)!' And there it was."

In an interview made for the behind the scenes video of

'Love Conquers All', Ian Paice said; "Joe's audition took basically about two minutes. You know, after that we were just having fun."

So, was Joe Lynn Turner a good choice for Deep Purple? Well, it is certainly a question that divides opinion rapidly. With three successful Rainbow albums to his credit (1981's *Difficult To Cure*, *Straight Between The Eyes* in 1982, and *Bent Out Of Shape* in 1983), he had certainly shown what he was capable of both as an individual musician and in terms of the creative rapport that he had already established working with Blackmore and Glover. By 1990, Ian Paice and Jon Lord were the only two members of MkII Deep Purple not to have played with Joe Lynn Turner.

Jon Lord told *Radio & Records* in November 1990; "It's tinged with sadness, this happiness at having a new album, because it doesn't contain Ian. But Joe's brought a snap and pizzazz to the band, and I really do hope the more old-fashioned Purple fans will accept it."

Colin Hart surmised his thoughts at the time in his autobiography; "Would it sell? Yes, to the hardcore fans, of which there were, thankfully, tens if not hundreds of thousands. Would it win new ones? The jury was out on that."

By 1990, there was arguably a maturity in Deep Purple's musicianship and certainly, in their approach to it. For instance, upon being asked, "At your age musicians prefer to hear a single note and not hundreds, right?" Blackmore told *Burrn* in November 1990; "Yes and no... Difficult question... Hmm, let me think... Well, I still don't follow what other guitarists are doing. In today's world it's all about playing fast and technical, but that just bores me. I don't follow that fashion, and I hope that there'll come a time when people will listen to guitarists, who are playing from the heart. These changes will become visible if you pay attention to the fact that Eric Clapton has become popular again; Jeff Healey, too. People are beginning to get bored of guitarists who are just paying attention to the speed and technique. Despite this, the shred guitar playing hasn't gone out of fashion, it might well get even more popular. I don't think it makes any sense. It's like reading Shakespeare's verses at double speed, but what's the point?"

Slaves And Masters was released in October 1990. Deep Purple's thirteenth album, it got to number eighty-seven in the US and to number forty-five in the UK. It got to number five in Switzerland where it went gold. Not bad going, but compared to the band's other albums, it was a far cry from previous successes — even *The House Of Blue Light* had got to number thirty-four in the US and to number ten in the UK.

In October 1990, it was considered in *Metal Hammer* that the Purple landscape looked something like this: "In the pantheon of British supergroups, Deep Purple stands alongside the giants — like Led Zeppelin, Black Sabbath and Yes. From their formative years in the seventies onwards, they have always created exciting, challenging music in which rock, blues, and even elements of classical music and jazz, fused together. Albums such as *Deep Purple In Rock*, *Machine Head* and *Who Do We Think We Are* have long been "essential" in any self respecting collection. And they have created some of the most enduring anthems of our time, from 'Smoke On The Water' to 'Black Night'. The band has seen many changes and upheavals, but it had invariably consisted of a bunch of powerful personalities revolving around the atomic core of Ritchie Blackmore, one of the most innovative, influential and respected guitarists in rock."

Yet Ritchie had a long period out of Purple when he led Rainbow from 1975 until the historic Purple reunion in 1984. *Perfect Strangers* was followed by *The House Of Blue Light*, but after a final live album from Polydor, they seemed to go into a freeze frame mode. They left Polydor, Ian Gillan was fired in 1989 and Blackmore was so unhappy it was rumoured that he would sooner revive Rainbow than continue with Purple. But after a year the band had a new singer, Joe Lynn Turner, who had worked with Ritchie in Rainbow and had recently quit Yngwie Malmsteen, after a tough time with the turbulent Swede.

With the new album, *Slaves And Masters*, together with the single, 'King Of Dreams' it looked like the nineties version of the classic band at last had the potential to really show the new generations what all the old excitement was about. They were confident of getting a hit single and promised to tour Europe extensively, as well as the States.

By some, *Slaves And Masters* is considered to be a weak Rainbow sound-alike. In particular, this is often considered to be the case on the basis of not only the line-up, but the fact that many advocate that in MkV Deep Purple, Blackmore had more control of the band because Ian Gillan wasn't there to challenge him.

Ian Gillan recalled in his 1993 autobiography, *Child In Time*; "*The House Of Blue Light* had been a struggle. Suggestions and half-worked ideas were strangled, but so long as Ritchie had been happy with the guitar parts, the lads were happy with the project. Well, fuck it, I wasn't happy, and I'd said so. Perhaps my own surrender took a different form, and I suppose there were times when my own way of dealing with frustration gave them the chance to think of me as a nuisance — and I certainly accept I know how to be that."

Apparently Blackmore wanted to have more control but nobody will ever truly know what went on unless they were there. Even accounts from the band's roadie, Colin Hart, are not going to be without some kind of bias.

Hart stated in his autobiography; "Roger and Ian would go ahead of the others to write the material. Two of them put together some reasonably impressive songs, but there was trouble-a-brewin'. Ritchie not only didn't like them, but from the moment the band reunited he had also wanted a change in the songwriting royalty agreement. Traditionally all Purple songs had been credited equally to the "band". Ritchie wanted this changed to the individual writers responsible for each song, irrespective of the collective work that was done on them to knock them into shape. This was as welcome as a fart in a spacesuit. These guys were a collective songwriting partnership in every sense of the word. I was there and saw the process evolve. Ian was always writing lyrics, always had a book with him where he constantly wrote down ideas based on his daily observations of his and life in general. Roger never stopped arranging in his head, thinking about how songs could always be improved. No Purple song would be the same without the input and musical brilliance of Jon and Paicey either. They were the energy that breathed life into them. Of course Ritchie was important, pivotal even to those stunning riffs that were the very essence of the band. In short, they were a *band*. A lot of problems occurred because nobody, apart from Ian, would ever directly confront Ritchie over such issues. Jon, Roger and Paicey could be unhappy with some aspects of the songs, but they would privately bitch to Ian, so to speak. The others preferred to load the gun, so long as Ian would fire it, which of course he was more than happy to do. They'd even go to Bruce with their problems who, in turn, would tell the guitarist that they were unhappy. Ritchie would reply truthfully that they had not told him there was a problem to which Bruce would just shrug and say, 'Well, they wouldn't.' However, the royalty question was just Ritchie being Captain Chaos again. He just loved it. Peace and tranquillity were just there for him to gleefully disrupt and he never missed an opportunity."

Interestingly, the way that any individual chooses to assess *Slaves And Masters* could plausibly be informed by their opinion of the Rainbow albums featuring Joe Lynn Turner as vocalist. For those who didn't like the AOR sound and the absence of Ronnie Dio, it is understandable as to why they were dreading the announcement of Turner being recruited as Deep Purple's frontman.

However, for those who enjoyed the melodic characteristics of Joe Lynn Turner era Rainbow, it is feasible that they may have been more welcoming of the news. The funk and soul influences of MkIII and MkIV aside, when fans thought of Deep Purple MkII, heavy rock is what often sprung to mind. It was certainly a far cry from the sound of Turner era Rainbow to many. Hmm, but what about songs like 'Fire Dance' from *Bent Out Of Shape* and 'Death Alley Driver' from *Straight Between The Eyes*?

Each to their own, but either way, it is understandable as to why the recruitment of Joe Lynn Turner to Deep Purple was met with a very mixed reception. Colin Hart asserted; "This version of Purple was too "poppy", it just wasn't the same band or importantly, the same sound. A lot of the press reviews said it was more like a Rainbow show than a hard rock Purple show."

In response to the question of whether he saw Deep Purple in the band's early days, Turner was quoted in *Metal Hammer* in October 1990; "Oh yeah, constantly. Our paths have crossed many times and if you believe in magic this couldn't be more cosmically perfect. As I say, I grew up on their music. I loved Ian's voice but I never tried to copy it. Certainly he was an influence but I don't have that type of voice. He does the oddball screaming stuff, whereas mine is more melodic and bluesy."

One song from the *Slaves And Masters* sessions was made for the 1990 film, *Fire, Ice And Dynamite*. Jon Lord didn't play on the song — it was performed by Turner, Blackmore, Glover and Paice. A hard rock song and not too different in sound to the material on *The House Of Blue Light*.

Notably though, the writing of the song is credited to Blackmore/Turner/Glover. Deep Purple went with that number when they were asked if they would be up for performing a different song that had been written by Harold Faltermeyer. Deep Purple's musical contribution to the film was released on the film's soundtrack CD.

It was reported in *Metal Hammer* in October 1990; "The band have also been working on a track for a movie called *Fire, Ice And Dynamite*, which shows how serious Purple are about working again. Their next step will be a tour. They hit the road in January but the dates are not confirmed yet. They will start rehearsals in England and will probably tour America first. Then they hope to play their first dates in the UK since 1987 when Ritchie broke his finger. At the time they were disappointed with the sales of their album and there didn't seem much point in carrying on touring. Purple are determined to make a bigger splash this time. The band have definitely updated their sound."

Upon its release, *Slaves And Masters* was met with a mixed reception from the music press. As for the fans, some of the complaints were in the lexicon that it was Deep Purple's worst album of all time. Some were angry that it sounded more like a Foreigner record than a Deep Purple one (which is ironic really; Blackmore was accused of "doing a Foreigner" in the eighties when he explicitly chose to take Rainbow in a more commercial direction).

Other frustrations from fans were that the lyrics were banal on tracks such as 'Fire In The Basement'. Many complained that *Slaves And Masters* was a far cry from the much-loved *Made In Japan* (1972). In fairness, people who wanted the heavy metal and the camera-smashing, Stratocaster-destroying aggression from Blackmore, were perhaps pretty pissed off that they didn't get it from Deep Purple's 1990 offering. After all, tracks like 'Fortuneteller' and 'King Of Dreams' weren't quite in the mould of "heavy metal" (was Deep Purple heavy metal though? Welcome to the debate of definitions and differences on heavy metal and hard rock, or whatever you want to call it. Still though, the fact is that in the eyes of many fans, *Slaves*

And Masters was certainly no *Machine Head* — it wasn't trying to be really but, well, some people were very unhappy about this!).

Turner was quoted in *Metal Hammer* in October 1990; "I come from a no-shit attitude and I hope I've given the band a kind of face lift. This is not 1972, and the guys don't want to rest on their laurels. They want to make records for 1990. I don't know if this album is "commercial" but it's certainly accessible. I think 'King Of Dreams' could be a hit, I really do. It's a groove song with a mystical type of feeling, it's sensuous and sexual. We did it all in one take, I swear. It doesn't scream to high heaven and it won't blow your ears off but it's got a really moody feeling... I can only say, I'm honoured. I know I've had some flak in the UK about being in the band. The old Purple fan clubs are very much rooted in the past, but if they really truly love this band they should give it the support to grow because it won't grow from the past. I'm not being arrogant but I do feel I can help bring Purple into the nineties."

Glover was quoted in the same feature; "People have said we sound like a nineties band, but on the other hand there are tracks that sound more like the real Deep Purple than any of the cuts on the last two albums, probably because it's much more live. Whatever Purple is — it's that mix of Ritchie's guitar sound and Jon Lord's organ sound. There will be purists who say it's not as good as it used to be but you can never compete with your past. People are scared of change, and when their favourite band changes people don't like it. I think we are capable of doing far more different things from what we do on this album. It's no bad thing to try something different. For example, Ritchie has a startling new guitar sound no one has heard before. It's very powerful but clean. I think he is playing better now than he has for five years. He is the kind of guitarist who could stretch out but he is quite content to remain within the bounds of a song. He'll play the rhythm part if need be, and doesn't want to try and impress people with his speed. But he does stretch out on the record. There's plenty of Ritchie solos!"

Musical comparisons aside, some fans just didn't like Joe Lynn Turner and didn't think that he was right for the job with Deep Purple. Possibly on the basis of the fact that he sounded so vocally different to Gillan, possibly because they didn't like his contribution to Rainbow. Who knows?

On balance though, no secret was ever made of the fact that the two singers were vocally very different in 1990 and certainly, it was something that was very much embraced when it came to the writing for *Slaves And Masters*; every singer brings something unique and wonderful to the table in their own way.

The opening track of 'King Of Dreams' certainly melds beautifully with Turner's voice. It is immensely melodic and really, it sets the scene for the fact that truthfully, a lot of the tracks on *Slaves And Masters* would certainly sound more at home on a Rainbow album than a Deep Purple one. Again, maybe a lot of this all comes down to how people felt about Turner-era Rainbow. 'Truth Hurts' is full of emotion and melodic rhythm in a way that is not too dissimilar to Rainbow's 'Can't Let You Go' from *Bent Out Of Shape*. 'Too Much Is Not Enough' also sounds more like a Rainbow song.

Despite the complaints of fans who wanted something heavier, it is certainly the case that 'Fire In The Basement' is performed by the whole band with energy and attitude and Blackmore's guitar is certainly biting on 'Wicked Ways'. Even with the melancholy of 'The Cut Runs Deep', there is a boisterous and heavy feel to the song. Paice's drums and Glover's bass really drive the song through and that is all alongside Blackmore's short — albeit sentimental sounding — guitar solo. 'Fortuneteller' is mysterious and engaging, with great keyboards from Jon Lord.

Sure, *Slaves And Masters* isn't full on hard rock, but does it have to be? Overall, it provides lots of variety and points of musical interest; it is very much the product of a band who sound creatively together. With 'Love Conquers All' being something of a power ballad, it is understandable as to why some may have felt that Deep Purple did a bit of a Spinal Tap in 1990. Hmm... Really though, the same debate that plagued the MkIV *Come Taste The Band* album springs to mind here. That is to say, with the line-up and stylistic changes taken into account, wouldn't it have been so much less pressure on everyone concerned not to go under the banner of Deep Purple? Surely by going by a different band name, it could have removed all of the connotations and thus expectations?

In response to the question of "Does it weigh heavily on your shoulders that you are now carrying the name of Deep Purple around like excess baggage?" Joe Lynn Turner was quoted in *Kerrang!* in March 1991; "Yeah, I do feel very pressurised, very much so, because it's just totally unnecessary. It feels very different being in the band because of the whole legend that surrounds the name. I don't think it's working for us, it's working against us. If we called it something different then there wouldn't have been any of these big comparisons between me and Gillan and all that crap. My attitude is fuck off, or fuck me off, or do anything you wanna do. Why bring it up? Don't buy the record, don't come to see us, goodbye. A rose by any other name would smell as sweet. Gillan said 'why not call it Rainbow?' but it's not Rainbow. There are four members of Purple, three members of Rainbow, two members of Whitesnake, so what is it? I didn't have much choice in the matter but if they'd asked me, I would have said that it would work against us. It's a younger market now, a younger audience, and people tend to look on Purple as dinosaurs — but as far as making records, playing live, and steaming ahead is concerned, the guys are as young as ever. They're playing with a passion that I haven't heard since *Machine Head*!"

Deep Purple - *Slaves And Masters*: In-depth

In response to the comment of "Isn't it fairly obvious that the legend of Deep Purple is essential in helping to put bums on seats, especially in America? I mean, look at Bad Company. They wouldn't mean anything if it wasn't for the name," Turner was quoted in the same feature; "That's probably true but Bad Company have had hits with Brian Howe in the band, albeit a Foreigner niche. Maybe I should have joined Foreigner instead! I think we'll do well whatever, but all this stuff is a pain in the ass. All I want people to do, and this is my statement, is just listen to the fuckin' thing, come and see us, make up your own mind — that's it. People's pre-conceived notions give you pressure. Why don't these people go and buy Gillan albums? Phone up Blackmore and ask him why it's called Purple!"

The trouble with being under the name of Deep Purple was that it presented pressures on all band members to subscribe to creating a style of music that they were not necessarily drawn to at the time. The name of Deep Purple came with connotations, a legacy and essentially, perhaps, restrictions. Imagine having lots of musical ideas and being presented with one of those "computer says no" moments? It was the same thing that largely inspired Blackmore to call it a day with Deep Purple in 1975 when he wanted more creative freedom (hence Rainbow), it was the same thing that made fans bemoan MkIV's *Come Taste The Band* in 1975 because it was driven by funk more than hard rock under the particular influences of David Coverdale, Glenn Hughes and Tommy Bolin.

Could it have been that the ball and chain of the Deep Purple name put *Slaves And Masters* at a disadvantage before many fans had even given it a chance? Turner told *Kerrang!* in March 1991; "Most people seem to say that it's a great record *in spite* of being a Deep Purple album! People want to trash it but they can't because it *is* a great album! Deep Purple fans should rally, like people do around a football team that changes its members from year to year. Sometimes people like the old centre forward, but it's the new guy who scores the most goals!"

For everything that the *Slaves And Masters* album isn't, there's probably a lot to be said for what it is in its own right.

Surely, it was imperative to band dynamics at the time that Gillan wasn't there? Rewind to the making of *The House Of Blue Light*. It was recorded in Stowe, Vermont and produced by Roger Glover with Nick Blagona responsible for the engineering. The general narrative relating to the days of making the album are that it was a difficult and stressful time for all concerned. So much so that in interviews, the album has been rarely spoken of in a positive light by any of those who were involved with it.

So much were Gillan and Glover's frustrations with working on *The House Of Blue Light* that they happily embraced the opportunity to work on an extra-curricular album to get the creative ideas out that they just didn't feel able to do under the messy band politics of Deep Purple at the time.

Colin Hart recalled in his autobiography; "Once the album was finished, Ian and Roger accompanied by Charlie Lewis and our Canadian engineer Nick Blagona went off to Montserrat in the Caribbean to do their own album, *Accidentally On Purpose*."

Gillan recalled; "It was not only a release valve after frustrations of the Purple session, but also the first time we'd had the chance to work on material unencumbered by the expectations and limitations of a band. We would just write songs. Songs that had their own value. We smoked a little ganja and started to relax. About half of the album was done but we had to stop as the next Purple tour was about to commence."

On balance, everyone in Deep Purple probably had the propensity — and perhaps even the explicit need — to be allowed the freedom the think outside the box. Blackmore was quoted in *Burrn* in November 1990; "I always hated to do what other people did, I never do what's expected of me. I would hate it if I would have to limit myself. I have always believed in going my own way. That's also why I didn't drive a car for a long time. Also everyone in the US is crazy about baseball, I personally prefer football (soccer), which isn't very popular over here. I love medieval and classical music... even in music, I try to stay away from the most popular things. That's my way of life... For example, if everyone around me is drinking beer, I would never drink it. I don't like to be like others. I prefer to be incomprehensible, not from this world... At school, everyone thought I was crazy. The difference now is that everyone became used to it. Also, many people think that a musician must be odd. But this strangeness isn't connected with music. I was already strange, before I became interested in any music."

Ian Gillan compared the making of *The House Of Blue Light* to the negative experiences he had whilst working on *Who Do We Think We Are* in 1972; "Rog and I did a great deal of preparation for what was to become *The House Of Blue Light*, only to find that, by now, Ritchie wasn't interested in listening to any of us... This was going to be a struggle, there was no cohesion, and it reminded me of the time in Rome, years before in 1972, when the circumstances were very similar as we tried to make *Who Do We Think We Are*. Ritchie hated a song called 'Painted Horse', and it was a war trying to get it released at all. Now we had the 'Mitzee Dupree' story, which I worked on with Rog, to give a lyric to one of the rough backing tracks. Ritchie hated it so much, he refused to re-record it, so what you hear on the album is the original demo. It's hard to deal with that sort of thing sometimes, and I didn't. It pissed me off big time... if the chemistry isn't right if the spirit isn't there, then an album can sound like a struggle. In my humble opinion, *Blue Light* and *Who Do We Think We Are* fall into that category."

Blackmore was quoted of *The House Of Blue Light* in *Burrn* in November 1990; "The recording of the album took us so long, that even before the release, I was already tired of it.

Why Slaves And Masters?

On this album, there wasn't even one successful song. During the recording sessions the problems already started with Ian Gillan. That's why it took us so much time to finish it. Within the group we constantly had conflicts, which made it very difficult. So when we finished recording the album, I said: 'I don't want to record another album in such an atmosphere.'... I think some of the songs were good, but I can't think of one that I really liked personally... I'm always interested in making music, but I don't like to spend so much time in the studio, working for days on just one song. I start to lose my interest and enthusiasm. Then I often ask myself: 'What am I doing here?' I like to play and write music when I feel like it, when I'm in the right mood. On *The House Of Blue Light* there aren't such songs. Besides, I also don't like the sound of the drums, which is also why I never listened to this record afterwards... I took it as a matter of course. The fact that we have spent so much time on this record, killed all the songs, they didn't sound natural anymore. A really good song is written in something like five minutes. When you listen to these songs, you will realise that some of them are actually not that bad, but the endless editing killed them."

Jon Lord told *Metal Hammer* in December 1990; "I think Ian slipped out of position during the last three months and went in an opposite direction. He never seemed to agree to a decision that we made. At least we came to the opinion — and not just Ritchie, don't believe that — that it was not worth it to carry on with him. The enjoyment factor in this band was so high — it's what I was doing the major part of my musical life with one holiday in Whitesnake that we didn't want to let the band go down this way... He wasn't giving us anything back. I don't want to criticise Ian as an artist. He is marvellous and I love him."

It was reported in *Kerrang!* in March 1991; "The specific circumstances surrounding Gillan's sacking had not yet been publically outlined by any of Purple until our interview, but it was generally known that the deed was done at a managerial level, with no member of Purple making personal contact with the singer."

When asked why things were done "so coldly", Jon Lord was quoted in the same feature; "I suppose a sense of embarrassment would be the best answer to that. We felt happier that our manager should do it. You'd call it, almost, cowardly, I suppose, if you wanted to be perfectly honest. It was only that we thought it would be cleaner... We felt that he (Gillan) was distancing himself more and more from the band. He had his own management, he refused to be managed by our manager. He was openly scathing about our manager. Contrary to what he believes, he was not sacked because he didn't like our manager. That's bullshit. We decided he should terminate his employment with us because we didn't think he was pulling in the same direction. It's a sad fact, but true."

Indeed, the facts surrounding Gillan's departure from Deep Purple were pretty hazy in the media at the time. He was quoted in the *Sandwell Evening Mail* in August 1990; "One of the reasons I was sacked from Deep Purple was that I wanted to tour but the rest of the band didn't. They wanted to spend two years making an album, which is ridiculous. I'd rather be singing than having time off — even after two months in the Caymans I can't wait to get back on the road... I suppose I am a workaholic, but I certainly enjoy everything I do."

The narrative that everyone in the band was unhappy during the recording of *The House Of Blue Light* was as public at the time as it remains today. Blackmore said to *Guitar* in March 2010; "I think I played like shit on it, and I don't think anyone else really got that into it. To me it was a bit of a disaster."

Jon Lord told *Modern Keyboard* in January 1989; "*House Of Blue Light* was a weird album and hard to put together. We made the massive mistake of trying to make our music current.

We discovered that people didn't want us to do that."

Promotional videos were done for the songs 'Bad Attitude' and 'Call Of The Wild'. Whilst *The House Of Blue Light* sold reasonably well, even Deep Purple themselves didn't have the highest expectations for it.

However, *The House Of Blue Light* was reviewed in *Rolling Stone* in February 1987; "Of the seventies hard-rock dinosaurs that still roam the earth, Deep Purple is one of the few with any credibility left in its crunch. *The House Of Blue Light* — the second album by Purple's classic *In Rock* line-up since their return to active duty — is certainly a marked improvement over their lukewarm '84 comeback, *Perfect Strangers*, and, except for a couple of outright duds on side two, is as good as this band has ever been since its 'Smoke On The Water' salad days. 'Bad Attitude' opens the album with five minutes of vintage *Machine Head* sludge — Ian Paice's thunder sticks calling the proceedings to order with a rigid goose-step beat, Ian Gillan raping his tonsils with the vigour of yesteryear. And 'Mad Dog' is basically an '87-model 'Highway Star', high-speed metal fortified with Jon Lord's lusty Hammond organ sound and the brass-knuckle guitar of Ritchie Blackmore."

"The band has spiked its old hammer-and-anvil sound with a little future tech here and there: 'The Unwritten Law' features subtly deployed electro-hand-claps and percolating sequencer amid its clenched-fist chorus and Blackmore's loco fretwork. But it's only when Purple turns on the retro-charm full blast that *The House Of Blue Light* really goes up in flames. 'Hard Lovin' Woman' and 'Dead Or Alive' are both body-slam rockers in the old blitzkrieg spirit of 'Speed King' and 'Fireball', while Paice's sledgehammer-of-the-gods drumming and Blackmore's punch-your-lights-out chords keep 'Call Of The Wild', with its atypically poppy hook, from turning into neo-Boston fluff."

"Fortunately, all that crash 'n' burn also obscures most of the album's lyric embarrassments. Although Gillan is hardly the Alan Alda of heavy metal, 'Mitzi Dupree', a heavy-plodding blues, may be a new low in rock-star sexism ('I said what is this queen of the ping pong business... I said ooh, have another drink...'). But aside from the rather purple poetry, the ho-hum Armageddon stomp 'Strangeways' and a notable lack throughout the album of classic Blackmore psycho-chicken-scratch soloing, *The House Of Blue Light* is a surprisingly strong return from the tar pits. There's no 'Smoke On The Water' here, but Deep Purple still has a pretty good fire going down below."

It seems the tour following *The House Of Blue* light was a dramatic one, and not for the right reasons. The problems ranged from significant injuries to pure slapstick violence. Blackmore broke his finger during a gig in Phoenix. He threw his Stratocaster in the air and caught it awkwardly. He managed to finish the show — with difficulty and in pain — but it ultimately resulted in all remaining tour dates being postponed until further notice.

Gillan and Glover used the postponement to their advantage and went to Minot Studio in New York and then the Power Station to finish *Accidentally On Purpose*, something that had also given them a break from the stresses of being in Deep Purple whilst on the road. Gillan asserted; "Although *The House Of Blue Light* wasn't going to set the world on fire, the tour started well and got better. Rog and I decided to take a bus while the other guys made their own arrangements. This would give us the chance to write some more stuff for *Accidentally On Purpose*, while cruising through the countryside and enjoying the scenery. No rush, no airports, no packing and unpacking, party when you want, sleep it off in your bunk. It's the only way to go."

And that was just the tip of the iceberg! Colin Hart recalled in his autobiography; "The show sounded good and looked good and Ian and Ritchie were being civil to each other. Jon

Lord had his separate case full of his reading matter for the tour, which would, over the next nine months, become the tour library and Ian had his *Daily Telegraph* crosswords, which, as he would assure a puzzled Steve Morse years later, was how he practised his craft of lyrics."

"Roger just took it all in, glad to be back on the road... Most of the time, dates end up a blur in your consciousness, but Richfield Coliseum, Cleveland on May 11th stood out as a day lifted from the mundane. Ritchie squished a plate of spaghetti into Ian's face on the pretext that the singer had somehow "spiked" it. Cool! Now Ian is not a small guy and I fully expected World War III to instantly break out as did Ritchie who put up his fists Queensbury Rules style, which on reflection now was hilarious as Ian would have just kicked him in the bollocks. No, Ian, seriously pissed off, but in wonderful and surprising control, got up imperiously, told the guitarist that fighting was not happening and disappeared into the bathroom to clean up, shutting the door behind him. Ritchie just stood there with all of us just looking at him stony-faced. I half expected someone to say that he should have had the carbonara instead. He went back to his room. The following show, understandably, was not the best they'd done."

Ian Gillan gave his account of the event in his 1993 autobiography; "One of the last memories of that tour is a dressing room incident after one of the British dates. The relationship between Ritchie and I simmered and was strained, and on one occasion it cracked. I was in the room when Ritchie burst in furious, a china dinner plate in his hand. On the plate was spaghetti, which someone had smothered in ketchup — given how things were between us I guess he assumed it was my doing. He raced over to me and said, 'Did you do this?', but before I could open my mouth, he smashed the plate into my face as if it were a custard pie. I slowly stood up, and he started dancing around me with his fists up saying 'Come on, then, come on.' I said, 'I don't want to hit you, Ritchie,' and turned and walked into the bathroom, where I cried with such rage and frustration and said, 'I quit.' I changed my mind within seconds as I realised how little it would achieve, and it was downhill all the way from there."

Despite the obvious tensions, Deep Purple still had a legacy to be proud of and one that they didn't shy away from embracing. The very album title of *The House Of Blue Light* paid homage to the lyric used in 'Speed King' from *In Rock*. The lyric was in reference to Little Richard's 'Good Golly Miss Molly', the line in itself having been taken from the 1946 song 'The House Of Blue Lights' composed by Don Raye and Freddie Slack. It had been a hit by Chuck Miller in 1955 and was also recorded by Chuck Berry, the same year (1958) that Little Richard scored a hit with 'Good Golly Miss Molly'.

By 1990, it is understandable as to why fans were cautious to embrace the fifth line-up of the band and indeed, any output from them. Inevitably though, this book is not an underdog story about the *Slaves And Masters* album; it is a celebration of some damn good music that stands up in its own right, no matter how it may or may not sit in Deep Purple's overall legacy. So at the risk of sounding a little hypocritical on the legacy front, I'll say this: "listen, learn, read on…" No, wait, scratch that… Deep Purple in 1990 were a very different band to what they had been before. And really, that's the point and largely, what *Slaves And Masters* seems to be about as an album.

When asked to compare *Slaves And Masters* to *In Rock*, Jon Lord said to *Metal Hammer* in December 1990; "It's two main differences. One is quite obviously the studio techniques, and the other one is less obvious. It is a personal opinion and it's the one major criticism I have of the album — I'm ninety five percent happy with it but this five percent is that it doesn't have a 'Speed King' on it. Or a 'Gypsy's Kiss'. Or a track like 'Burn'… I'm happy and the songs are fine in their current order.

Why Slaves And Masters?

I would just like to add one number. We had a number with a double-bass drum, the same tempo as 'Fireball'. I loved it and Ian Paice loved it too, but we were in the minority. If it were on *Slaves And Masters*, I think the balance would be better."

The announcement of *Slaves And Masters* was a met with anticipation. It was reported in *Cash Box* in September 1990; "On October 9th, RCA is scheduled to release a new album by one of the most influential bands of the sixties and seventies, Deep Purple. The seminal band's line-up on *Slaves And Masters* includes Ritchie Blackmore on guitar, Roger Glover on bass, Joe Lynn Turner on vocals, Ian Paice on drums and Jon Lord on keyboards. Although 'Smoke On The Water', 'Highway Star', 'Burn' and other Deep Purple classics had a definite influence on heavy metal and hard rock, headbanging is only part of the Purple legacy. An advance cassette of the diverse *Slaves And Masters*, which Glover produced, exposed this headbanger to its first single, the haunting 'King Of Dreams', the slow, eerie 'Fortuneteller', mid-tempo non-metal like 'Breakfast In Bed' and scorching yet melodic rockers such as 'Fire In The Basement' and 'Wicked Ways'. *Slaves And Masters* is Deep Purple's first album since 1987's *House Of Blue Light*, which went gold in the US."

Turner was quoted in *Metal Hammer* in October 1990; "We've got some socio-political things, some early, early root Purple with 'Breakfast In Bed' which is really cool. 'Truth Hurts' is a kind of special performance for me too."

By the early nineties, a lot of young rock fans were keen to get their heavy metal fix and in many ways, Deep Purple operated very much outside of that niche. In an interview with Japanese radio in 1991, in response to the question of, "Most of the old bands like Sabbath and Heep are declining now, so Purple is quite an important survival now, do you agree?" Ian Paice replied, "What we have in hard rock at the moment is a very limited perspective of what rock is all about. From the

Deep Purple - *Slaves And Masters*: In-depth

heavy metal and thrash thing it's quite limited in what they're trying to do. What they do is just one bit of what we were doing, what Zepp and Sabbath did. The picture is bigger than that, there's room for a lot more variety in hard rock, different emotions, so I find it now a little limiting. If somebody can be around from the late sixties, early seventies period and, I don't want to sound big headed, but show them how it should be done. If we stop, all this knowledge seems to disappear and it will stay narrow and confined. It would be nice if Zepp could be around. It's great that Pink Floyd is still around. Dave Gilmour has a wonderful grasp of what is right *for now*."

In response to the question of "What do you think of the rock scene these days with all the different variations of thrash and heavy metal?" Jon Lord said to *Metal Hammer* in December 1990; "I think it's probably very healthy and it's going to be healthier as we get into the nineties. I like the enthusiasm of the metal bands and it's interesting to me that hard rock in general sells more concert tickets than just about any other kind of music. What does that tell us? I think it tells us that it's unpretentious, vital, unambiguous, exciting, hard — it's everything a music fan could want, except maybe subtle."

When asked "Does a band like Deep Purple have a place in today's rock scene?" Lord was quoted in the same feature; "Absolutely! It's a place we earned by being here! It's not a question of us moving out of the way to let people pass. It's 'catch me if you can!' We are still on the road and the road is wide enough. We are not standing in anybody's way. When it's time for us to get off the road we'll know immediately because we'll get told. We want to play and everybody who wants to play can play. There are no rules that say 'after twenty two years you have to go.' That's like you saying, 'it's time to kill your grandfather because he's been here for eighty-eight years.' That's not the way it works!"

The interviewer perhaps wasn't convinced (either that or

they were playing devil's advocate!) and proceeded to ask: "Dicky Peterson from Blue Cheer, who started out with you in the sixties, recently said in an interview that it was impossible for reformed bands like Deep Purple to project the same feeling that you used to," to which Lord responded; "Bullshit! I'm sorry, Dicky, but I don't agree with you, that's what I mean to say. I had one of the best years of my life when we reformed in '84. I had a marvellous time. It was a different feeling because it was a feeling as if we moved on but it wasn't worse. And so to say it was impossible to have that feeling again, to me, doesn't make sense."

In an interview with *Burrn* magazine in November 1990, Blackmore was asked, "I don't know if you are aware of this band, but I love the new band Cinderella — their music has something and I think they have a good musical taste. What do you think about shredders who play from the heart, and those who do it just for the sake of speed?" His response: "I don't really know much about them. Of course, they are on the radio all the time, but it seems to me that the music always repeats itself in a circle, and when some kind of fashion reaches the end point, the music starts to strive for the opposite. In addition, if we talk about music that comes from the heart, then, for example, the Japanese people are always open for any kind of music. They are always listening very carefully, and I think they understand it. So, instead of following speed, they are enjoying music that comes from the heart. I think the shred guitar is mainly an American fashion, but the Americans have another positive side. When Americans become your fans, they stay with you for years, even decades. Meanwhile people from the UK have a new favourite band every six weeks. In America, a band's popularity is growing like a snowball, so that's a good place in a sense."

There was certainly a lot of variety in the world of rock music in the days of the *Slaves And Masters* album. When

Deep Purple - *Slaves And Masters*: In-depth

Metal Hammer published their reader's charts singles and albums list for January 1991, it included a broad mixture of bands, both those who had cut their careers in the sixties and seventies as well as those who were flying the flag for eighties and nineties hair metal; Black Sabbath, Led Zeppelin, Status Quo, Iron Maiden, Cinderella, Anthrax and Megadeath. Deep Purple were included amongst that list with their single, 'King Of Dreams'.

The record company had high hopes for the album. RCA's VP of Promotion, Butch Waugh, was quoted of *Slaves And Masters* in *Hitmakers* in October 1990; "the biggest album since the band got back together."

In the same article, it was reported that 200,000 albums had been pressed so far but that more would need to be done in view of the fact that the label planned to give Deep Purple a big promotional push for the top forty later that month.

Turner told *Metal Hammer* in October 1990; "Everybody is buzzing in the States about our record. They think it's gonna be big! I think it's a great album but I don't wanna count my chickens before they are hatched. Deep Purple is a musical melting pot but when it comes to the stuff I have to wrap my tonsils around they pretty much leave it up to me and Roger to sort out the songs and lyrics. You can't sing stuff you don't believe in."

The optimism wasn't misplaced considering the high esteem that the name of Deep Purple was held in. It was considered in *Guitar Magazine* in December 1990; "All the diverse sounds that had been germinating in British rock and progressive idioms came to well-integrated fruition in that music of Deep Purple. Electric blues, twentieth century modernism and aleatory sci-fi effects, classical jazz and ethnic tangents, allusions to funk and R&B, plenty of straight-ahead, loud rock 'n' roll, offset by toe-tapping pop tracks, not to mention telltale elements from the incipient heavy metal school — they employed it all. With an uncanny ability, and an ease and conviction that belies the magnitude of such an undertaking, Purple established themselves not only as a legendary band in rock history, but as the foundation for an immense musical dynasty which engendered countless progeny, touched the work of their colleagues past and present, gave rise to the fertile Euro-metal movement, and has shown no sign of abating more than two decades later."

A quick reality check is probably of value here as in, for all the dramatic accounts of what went wrong and what went right, the fact is that Deep Purple were still going out of choice, not duress. Colin Hart recalled; "With Deep Purple once again settled (well, for now at least. I never considered anything permanent), writing and rehearsals began for the next album, which would become *Slaves And Masters*. When they had reformed six years earlier, at one time or another they had all said that if one was to go they would call it a day, but when it came down to it, they wanted to carry on."

Jon Lord said in *Metal Hammer* in December 1990; "I'm damned sure we'll know when to stop. We aren't in the band to fulfil some contracts. We carry on because we want to and it's a great enjoyment to do. And there's no need to carry on for money. We're not multimillionaires but we do okay."

In such regard, artistically, they perhaps had more freedom than many. It would possibly be irrational to consider any Deep Purple album made between 1984 and 1993 to be *that* much of a hardship but on balance, it's all relative of course. Well, whether the individuals concerned were happy to be on the ride or not, either way, in 1990, the fans were given something to wrap their heads around, for better or for worse.

Deep Purple - *Slaves And Masters*: In-depth

Chapter Two
The Making Of Slaves And Masters

Even before the line-up of Deep Purple that came to be known as MkV was finalised, preparations for the next studio album started taking place. Colin Hart recalled in his autobiography; "Once back in America the months rolled by as many names were thrown into the ring for the singer's seat. Australians John Farnham and Jimmy Barnes being right up front with dear old Ronnie James Dio and Bad Company's Brian Howe. Ritchie called me up and said that the decision over a new singer would have to wait and I should go and find a new place to rehearse and record. Now this was late November and as per usual the location specification was 'Vermont, near a pub with a place where I can make a lot of noise close by to a condo complex, which we can all call home'."

"I eventually found a mothballed golf clubhouse in a remote part of Vermont in Stratton. 'This is winter and golf itself is not an option, so why not hire the place out to us fine English musicians,' I proposed to the owners. They accepted, quite bemused. The nearest airport worthy of the name was Albany in upstate New York, a hundred mile or so round trip, which was fine in the summer, but this was the depths of winter in arse-high snow. The band assembled, we began in earnest to contact singers and, where necessary, flew them in. Yup, to Albany which meant me driving back and forth through all weathers to pick 'em up and bring 'em in. Three such singers were American Terry Brock from a band called Strangeways, Jimi Jamison from Survivor and Kal Swann from

British rockers Lion. None made the grade except Jimi who, on his management's advice, turned us down in favour of a solo career. Finally Ritchie suggested Joe Lynn Turner, who was contacted and agreed to fly up. I met him at Albany and in atrocious weather took him to golf! It took hours and on arrival I asked him if he minded going straight in to meet the band and go through a few numbers. Joe, as I've said earlier, was and still is the consummate professional, and was not fazed by this at all. He stepped right up to the plate and strutted his stuff. Smiles all round, one singer delivered. The scene was surreal. Here was the band muffled up in winter gear in this bar overlooking rolling hills of deep snow with a tennis court just visible in a large drift outside. The heating was struggling to be worthy of the name, but at least the bar was open."

So what was Joe Lynn Turner doing when he got the call from Deep Purple? He told *Kerrang!* in March 1991; "I've always said to the others that it's going to take nine months to a year of education and repair. I knew that when I got the offer to join the band, but I immediately felt that there was some energy here. To be part of a legend is appealing, but this is harder work than I was doing before. I had Al Petrelli on guitar and James Kottak on drums. It was a good-looking, good-playing, piss-off kinda band, but then Purple called me and Alice Cooper called Al. He had a daughter on the way and you can't sniff at five to six grand a week, so we put the band on ice. It doesn't bother me. I've been in enough bands not to bother. Nothing bothers me after Yngwie. I put my heart and soul into that band but he's a fuckin' bastard. By the way, he never fired anyone. We all left... *Odyssey* was his best album ever and I just regard it as a good life and musical experience. It toughened me up for this job. I've got a shirt that reads, 'You can't intimidate me. I toured with Yngwie!' It's like 'Take you best shot pal, I'm immune!'"

It was reported in *Metal Hammer* in October 1990;

"Although rumours had been raging all this year about the future of Purple, it seems the decision to invite Joe into the band was taken last December. After he sorted out his own business affairs he joined the band and quit the snows of Vermont for the sunshine of Orlando, Florida, to begin rehearsals and work on the new album. Come January the band began recording in a video studio in a kind of "rehearsal situation" without the use of headphones. The idea was to keep the spontaneity of the original jams with Joe."

To which Roger Glover was quoted, "We kept going until we got a live spontaneous take. We actually did the recording with a blanket over the control room window, so didn't feel there was a control room there. It became the symbolic blanket!"

The feature continued, "They produced tons of songs and riffs, much more than was actually used on *Slaves And Masters*. The LP got its name from the use of the twenty-four track digital machines, one of which is always referred to as the "master" and the other the "slave" and they are linked to produced forty eight tracks. A blackboard was set up containing album title suggestions but *Slaves And Masters* was the final choice."

Blackmore was quoted in *Burrn* in November 1990; "The name *Slaves And Masters* comes from the nicknames we gave the recorders in the studio. But the audience comes up with other explanations, one sees a sexual content, some people think it's politically motivated, feminists see it as a battle of the sexes. As for the cover, the crystal ball is in someone's arms controlling everything that is inside the ball. Besides, life is so unpredictable and mysterious that we can't even be sure of what we are today."

It was in late 1989 that Joe Lynn Turner was welcomed into Deep Purple following six months of trying to find a replacement for Ian Gillan. It was a successful jam on the song, 'Hey Joe', that sealed the deal. A sensible choice in many ways considering that Glover and Blackmore had already worked with Turner in Rainbow.

In response to the mention of the rumour that Rainbow would reform, Glover said in *Metal Hammer* in October 1990; "Oh there's been lots of rumours about everything. There was never any truth to that. In fact, we used to read the rumours for fun to find out what we were supposed to be doing. There must be a rumour factory somewhere. I was totally against it because I could see what the critics would say. It felt wrong. But then — we were stuck and Ian Paice and Jon Lord had not had the opportunity of working with Joe and had barely met him. So we agreed to have a jam with him. We were rehearsing in a golf club — it sounds very posh. In fact it was a wooden hut in a field in Vermont in the middle of winter. We had taken over the bar area and had all our gear set up, which was very handy because after we had finished a song we could go and have a drink."

"Joe walked in and said 'hi'. The first thing we did was 'Hey Joe' which Ritchie kicked off. The band started jamming and it felt absolutely great. It felt like the band wasn't rudderless anymore. And Joe sang absolutely brilliantly. His voice has matured a lot and he had more control. If he was guilty of anything in the past it was not having his own voice. He'd sound like the singers he admired. But his stint with Malmsteen and stuff on his own had helped him mature and he sounds like him now, not anybody else. After a couple of hours jamming we started writing — there and then. Then we had a meeting, sitting round the fireplace, and I had to say something, as I'd been so against him. I said, 'Well, I've gotta tell you, Joe just blew me away.' And from that moment I thought, damn the critics, listen to the music because he is making the band make music again."

In response to the rumours of a Rainbow reform, Turner told *Metal Hammer* in October 1990; "Yeah, there were rumours, and it was true. It was very possible because Ritchie wasn't sure what he wanted to do. He could either do Purple, or Rainbow, or a blues band, or a solo instrumental type thing. He wasn't really sure but now he's in the best of all possible positions because he's got a singer of his choice, and he's got the songs and melodies he wanted, and the band that he loves. He's a happy guy! And I think the playing on the album is very inspired. He's perking up. He got a bit drab for a while, now he feels 'Yeah, play that shit!' He's my favourite guy and I know when he's down, and right now he's up."

Despite some initial reluctance, there were many reasons as to why Turner was a good choice of singer for what would become Deep Purple MkV. Upon being asked, "Why did you decide on an established singer like Turner instead of like in 1973 when you decided to hire the unknown clothes trader David Coverdale?" Jon Lord said to *Metal Hammer* in December 1990; "A good question. Well, we did try. But we had one major problem — we are a band of a certain age and most of the singers we got audition tapes from were guys of twenty to twenty-two years. And two things would happen if we took a guy of that age. One — it would look wrong. And two — the poor guy would not stand the chance. So much collective experience around him and a young man of maybe twenty-two years our junior having to come in and try and control the band from the front like a singer must do to an enormous degree, that wouldn't have worked. I promise you we listened to thousands of tapes, some very good and some we passed on to other agencies saying, 'you should listen to this guy.' The problem was to find someone who looked right. It had to be someone at least thirty. It had to be someone of a certain type. So that was the major problem. We tried Jimi Jamison from Survivor and he fitted in great but then his management didn't want to do it. Then we had discovered a session singer called Terry Brock. A fabulous singer — but no magic, no sparks! In December of last year we were sitting front row of a large log fire and didn't know what to do now. Is this the end of it? Then Ritchie said, 'I'm really hesitant to say this but why don't we ask Joe to come and at least try?' So we did. And it was magic." So was David Coverdale even considered for the job? Apparently not. Jon Lord was quoted in the same feature; "No. That never came up. David has gone somewhere else and is doing his American Whitesnake. But now we've got an American singer as well and so the result is maybe similar."

Upon being asked who he preferred to work with out of Ian Gillan and Joe Lynn Turner, Blackmore was quoted in *Burrn* in November 1990; "It's very different... I like to work with Joe. For example, if it's snowing outside, we sit by the fire, I play the guitar and Joe starts to sing... That's how we work. Robert Plant once told me that Led Zeppelin recorded their tracks for *Kashmir* in seven minutes. Then Jimmy Page told Robert Plant to think about what to sing. We worked in the same way with Ian Gillan. We didn't write music together. He asked us to send him the tracks, when they're ready, so that he could write the lyrics."

"But Joe was involved in the whole process. For example, I would ask him: 'What's sounding better — should we play it in D or E?' and so on... We've worked out a lot of arrangements together. It was much easier to work with Joe. Ian very rarely listened to our writing sessions, he just felt responsible for the lyrics. It was very pleasing to work with Joe, because we worked together and exchanged a lot of ideas. So, perhaps, I prefer to work with him to answer your question."

In response to the question of "After the reunion there's a lot more exotic oriental scales in your playing. Is there any special reason for that?" Blackmore replied; "Not really. When I write songs, I just play the first thing that comes to my mind. There's a song, which isn't on the album, but it has elements of Japanese music. I try to write music within ten to fifteen minutes. I don't like working on a song for three days,

I want to keep it natural. I also think that the name of a song is very important for the listener. It creates an image in people's heads. If a song is called something like 'Crystal Ball', it creates mystical images in the head. That's why I'm interested in psychic research, I want to understand how people think. You might know that I've been doing this kind of research for almost twenty years, so sometimes when I listen to someone's speech, I wanna know: 'How does this guy really feel now? Is he honest?'."

Slaves And Masters was recorded in early 1990. Ian Gillan had actually done demos for some of the tracks that Deep Purple MkV began working on. In fact before the last few gigs with Gillan in September 1988, an excited Jon Lord told Purple biographer Jerry Bloom that they had already written four songs for the next album, one of which Lord said was his idea.

It was reported in the *Asbury Park Press* in April 1990; "Word is that the guys in Deep Purple have finished recording their latest album and are currently rehearsing in Florida. Purple's office would neither confirm nor deny the rumours that Joe Lynn Turner will be replacing Ian Gillan as lead vocalist… All we could squeeze out of Purple's office was a lame 'We're not ready to make an announcement at this time'."

Overall, *Slaves And Masters* was born out of relaxed studio jams. Glover told the *Asbury Park Press* November 1990; "There's a more live feel to it. I've always noticed that rehearsal tapes feel like they're much more fun than the finished product. By the time we've written the song, and distilled it, and got in the studio and put headphones on, and got the sound all cleaned up, it doesn't have the same impact as that time when you do something. It feels great. So, I've always wanted to capture that. This is coupled with the fact that Ritchie plays stuff, and he doesn't know what he's playing. He plays something, and you say: 'Aw, that's great! What was that?' And he goes: 'I don't know. What'd I do?' And the moment's gone. So, I wanted to create an atmosphere in which we were, in fact, recording rehearsals. Which is pretty much what we did."

Joe Lynn Turner said in the same feature; "We tried to do this album very live, I mean, 'King Of Dreams' was a jam. We never even knew we had it until three weeks later. We wrote a song over it and the guys walked in after the break and said: 'What's this? Is this us, or is this a new band?' We said, 'Well, this is your new single!' 'Truth Hurts' was another jam. 'Fire In The Basement' reminds me completely of old Purple. Sort of a 'Lazy' thing. It's clearly under the name "Deep Purple". With that heading, we have significant legends and attitudes to keep up."

Blackmore told *Guitar World* in February 1991; "I never work out my leads. Everything I do is usually totally spontaneous. If someone says, 'That was good; play that again,' I'm not able to do it. The only solo I've committed to memory is 'Highway Star'. I like playing that semitone run in the middle."

Jon Lord commented; "A lot of what we need for a song goes down on the tape when we put it down because of the musical ability of the members which is still very good… It's a straightforward album and very live. We played all together. We even had some troubles mixing as we had a little bit of leakage from one track to another but we can live with that because we get a better live feeling. We didn't want to put anything on the album that we couldn't play live. Now it's up to us to choose how much of that album will go into the stage show. And you get a better deal if we do it like that."

It is almost as if there was a "back to basics" philosophy in place. In an interview with Japanese radio in 1991, Ian Paice said, "What we realised was that we sort of got lost in the technology of the eighties, trying to do things we weren't good at and other people were — making super high quality technical records at the expense of the performance. On *Slaves*

And Masters we made a conscious effort to start making records again like we did twenty years ago. All be in a room, play it together and try and get it right! I think we got about fifty percent of that back, the next one will be even more live and hopefully the sound will reflect that more. The magic is getting five people to perform at the same time. The prime example is *Made In Japan*. By today's standards, it's not brilliant quality, but that's not important. The atmosphere and emotion of the night is still obvious to people who listen."

The relaxed methods used to create *Slaves And Masters* were such that it resulted in an album that sounds less laboured than *The House Of Blue Light*. Deep Purple themselves keenly advocated in interviews at the time that *Slaves And Masters* was an enjoyable album to make and a constructive phase of their musical creativity. So much so that in August 1990, *Radio & Records* quoted Roger Glover as having described the album as "the closest we've come to sounding like Deep Purple in many years."

Colin Hart recalled in his autobiography; "Roger was to produce the album and it consisted of working up new and exciting material... The atmosphere was relaxed and the recording was one of a series of jams... As was usual, it was tweaked by Roger at Soundtec and Power Station Studios in New York a little later, once the dust had settled and Roger could hear it all afresh. Nick Blagona assisted him."

As an album, *Slaves And Masters* is the product of a period in Deep Purple's tenure where tensions in the band didn't seem to evoke conflict and aggressions. Whether or not that was to the musical advantage or detriment of the album is very much subject to opinion. Whilst Deep Purple themselves may have enjoyed having a break from their working process being dominated by tensions between Blackmore and Gillan, a number of fans may have been disappointed that in many ways, *Slaves And Masters* is a lot more laid back than the two

MkII albums that bookend it, *The House Of Blue Light* and *The Battle Rages On...*

The style of the music on *Slaves And Masters* is a clear indication that a lot of the ideas on it came from the Rainbow trio of Blackmore, Glover and Turner. Still though, Lord's excellence on keyboards is very much at the fore, as is Paice's driving use of heavy drumbeats.

In response to the question of "How does this edition of Deep purple differ from past formations?" Blackmore told *Guitar World* in February 1991; "Musically, I would say the singer doesn't drink as much. But seriously, the older I get, the more I want to hear melodies. We really worked hard on constructing good, memorable songs and interesting chord progressions. That's what excites me at the moment. It also helped that our new singer, Joe Lynn Turner, writes and sings great melodies. With Joe, we didn't have to rely as much on heavy riffs. When I was twenty, I didn't give a damn about song construction. I just wanted to make as much noise and play as fast and as loud as possible."

Slaves And Masters has a lot going for it in terms of the fact that Turner brought a renewed energy and enthusiasm to Deep Purple at the time. The nucleus of Blackmore, Glover, Lord and Paice had been going through the motions on the last album they made with Ian Gillan as vocalist. That of course, is nobody's fault in particular — each to their own and all that.

But the fact is that in terms of MkV Purple's working process, a change was perhaps as good as a rest. There is a lot of high energy and enthusiasm across the whole of *Slaves And Masters*. On balance though, the AOR style of hard rock perhaps comes across that way naturally in comparison to the more blues orientated style of hard rock more associated with MkII. That's not to say that *Slaves And Masters* is without blues references though, but they are certainly less present on the album than the melodic style of pop rock that is more associated with Turner era Rainbow than the overall signature sound of Deep Purple.

Prior to joining forces with Deep Purple, Joe Lynn Turner had worked with Yngwie Malmsteen. He was candid about the fact that he hadn't enjoyed this phase of his career on a personal level and it is plausible that both creatively and in terms of working dynamics, the opportunity to work with his former bandmates from Rainbow was something to look forward to after working with the apparently difficult Yngwie.

When asked about his time with Yngwie Malmsteen, Turner said to *Metal Hammer* in October 1990; "It could have been something that really clicked. I thought the album was great. It was an exciting time but then it slowly reversed itself because of personality problems I guess. I don't know if you want to call it problems or just personality. Yngwie started a rumour that I was out of Purple, which I'm still pissed about. I got that from the horse's mouth and I don't know why he should say things like that. I only wish him well but my time with him started out happily then turned into a complete and utter nightmare. Why? Oh, he's impossible... He says one thing and does another. I just couldn't deal with him... He's obnoxious to everyone. It wasn't a personal thing. If anything, I got more respect because the record company wanted me there and he felt honoured to have somebody there who sang with Blackmore. It wasn't just me — he took the piss out of everyone. It's just his nature. He thinks he's gotta produce, he's got to write everything, he's gotta lead, and that people only come to see him, and they don't come to see the band."

It was reported in the same feature; "After leaving Yngwie Malmsteen, Joe spent some time in New York putting his own band together with guitarist Al Pitrelli who later went on to join Alice Cooper's band."

To which Turner said, "We had some great material, which I've now given away to other people. I had James Kottak on drums and Brad Gillis from Night Ranger lined up. We recorded a slew of songs on demo tape but then I had the call from Purple and that all fell apart. I looked at myself and asked, 'do you want to be in a legendary band?' I'd have to be mad to say no! It was a dream come true for me, and fantastic karma. I'd kept in touch with Ritchie over the years, and two years ago he was thinking of doing a Blackmore blues band as a one off, when that Gillan/Glover album came out. Then all of a sudden I had a call about Purple. They had other singers lined up. They had one guy who shall remain nameless, who is still a friend of mine. But I came in at the eleventh hour and started jamming on 'Hey Joe', 'Smoke On The Water' and 'Highway Star' and we had so much fun with it, we wrote 'The Cut Runs Deep' on the spot. Everyone was knocked out. When I got home the message was on my answer phone — 'You're in the band if you want it'."

The opening track 'King Of Dreams' is a fascinating statement for what is to follow on the rest of the album. It has a memorable chorus and melodic hooks that are attention grabbing. It is a mellow rock song based on a solid bass guitar groove. The whole song is powerful and soulful. It is AOR friendly but arguably this is not to its detriment musically. Upon being asked, "As a guitarist, what were you looking to do differently on this new record? For instance, the solo on 'King Of Dreams' has an exotic tinge that doesn't appear in any of your previous work," Blackmore replied in *Guitar World* in February 1991; "I wanted that solo to evoke a certain mood. It isn't meant to be a pointless exercise in speed; that's why it's very sparse. I was trying to make it an extension of the vocal melody and have it express something that was connected to the bloody song. I didn't want to just show off some trick I'd learned at the music store on Saturday morning."

As a guitarist Blackmore complemented Turner's intentions. The former said in *Burrn* in November 1990; "Of course, the melody is a very important aspect, and his (Joe Lynn Turner's) voice is perfect for that. When we worked with Ian, I thought more about the riffs. Now it's the opposite — we've concentrated more on the vocal lines now. On the other hand, some of the songs Ian Gillan sung just perfectly, and Joe has some problems with these. Joe is a very melodious singer, sometimes too melodic. So in this case, he has to adapt to these songs. Ian sang very aggressively and he shouted a lot. He was a totally different vocalist. He has his own style."

The Network Forty reviewed the 'King Of Dreams' single in October 1990; "Deep Purple's presence on Rock Radio spans nearly three decades, and now they are reformed, revitalised, and on the rise again with the release of 'King Of Dreams'. In its first week out, this single from the band's soon to be released *Slaves And Masters* album was the number one most added record at Rock Radio. Deep Purple is the band that arguably defined the hard rock genre. With their inclusion of a new lead vocalist Joe Lynn Turner, they have recaptured the energy and inspiration of years past. Of course, Deep Purple still includes guitar master Ritchie Blackmore and founding member Roger Glover. It's back to basics time, and Deep Purple is leading the way, twenty-two years after their first hit, 'Hush', went top five on the pop charts."   Well, there's no denying some of the inaccuracies in the review; Roger Glover wasn't a founding member of the band — MkI consisted of Nick Simper on bass and it was he who contributed to the band's first hit, 'Hush'. Inaccuracies aside, what matters here is that it didn't take a hardcore Deep Purple fan to appreciate the merits of the band's output for 1990.

Jon Lord's keyboard solo sparkles on 'The Cut Runs Deep', as does the piano introduction that he plays; the melodic structure of it is not too dissimilar to the pattern in Bach's *Toccata And Fugue In D Minor* whereby the entire melody bounces off the lowest note in the phrase (in this case, B).

Now, whilst making a reference to Bach does not a good piece of music make, does it suggest that there is a lot to be enjoyed about this track? Absolutely! Why? Because in terms of music theory, it's clear that a good amount of thought has gone into it. This is only my observation based on the band score (published in 1991 by Watanabe, ISBN4-8108-3746-7) rather than something Deep Purple put forward themselves in interviews but the fact is that, upon analysis from a music theory perspective, there are many musical moments in *Slaves And Masters* that support what Deep Purple said in interviews at the time about the enthusiasm they had for making the album.

In terms of Blackmore's reputation for being able to put forward an emotional solo, the one he does on 'The Cut Runs Deep' ranks right up there. It is short but melancholic. 'The Cut Runs Deep' just has an overall feel to it that is suggestive of the idea that, perhaps, Deep Purple were working well together at the time. In response to the interviewer's comment of "Jon Lord plays more textures, rather than actual lines, on this new album," Blackmore was quoted in *Guitar World* in February 1991; "Jon likes to see what I'm going to do and he enhances that. He's not a leader; he likes to follow."

'Fire In The Basement' is in the style of a classic blues based rock and it has all of the features that are not too far removed from a MkII song. So much so that it wouldn't be difficult to imagine Ian Gillan singing it. It contains Lord's sweeping use of the Hammond organ, and Blackmore's guitar figures are idiosyncratic of Deep Purple's signature sound. Lyrically, 'Fire In The Basement' isn't subtle but it certainly isn't trying to be either. It is full of innuendo in the style of 'Knocking At Your Back Door' and is a little reminiscent of 'Lazy' in how it is a very upbeat shuffle (something that reviewers often noticed in their accounts of the live shows from the 1991 tour — more on that in the next chapter).

In response to the question of "'Fire In The Basement'

has the same kind of rhythm like 'Lazy' or 'Starstruck'. Do you like to play the shuffle?" Blackmore answered in *Burrn* in November 1990; "Not that much. In 1964-1965, everything I played was a shuffle. Shuffle comes from the US, so this rhythm is more suited to the Americans. But it seems to have got a little bit out of fashion. So when we want to play something classical or old-fashioned at the rehearsals, we're always joking: 'Well, should we do a shuffle?' Of course playing everything in this rhythm would be boring. But of course there are exceptions, for example, I like the way Jimi Hendrix used this rhythm in 'Manic Depression'. Today's musicians don't like to use rhythms that you can't dance to. Record companies also have problems with that. We are fortunate to work with a record company and manager, which give us a lot of freedom in this regard. I'm happy about that. Most of today's rock bands have to sound like Guns 'n' Roses."

In *Metal Hammer* in December 1990 Jon Lord said; "I think a song like 'Fire In The Basement' is a really straight rocker with Ritchie's guitar on the one hand and the organ on the other. Another band wouldn't do a song like that. It's very much Deep Purple!"

'Fire In The Basement' was reviewed in *Billboard* in December 1990; "Second helping from (the) classic rock band's current *Slaves And Masters* set is a rollicking, blues-drenched headbanger. A natural for album rock radio, though top forty should jump aboard as well."

Even as a slow track, 'Truth Hurts' still dishes out a good serving of hard rock with a side of captivating melody. 'Breakfast In Bed' sounds very similar to a Bad Company track, something that didn't go unnoticed by many.

As a ballad, 'Love Conquers All' doesn't have any immensely distinguishing features in terms of melodic hooks but it is certainly not without its magic either. A decent track full of added dimension in the form of Blackmore's guitar contribution. He told *Burrn* in November 1990; "We've decided to play the intro with a keyboard, because I've forgotten how to play the cello."

The 'Love Conquers All' single was reviewed in *Billboard* in March 1991; "Classic rockers delve into their current *Slaves And Masters* album and pull out (a) power ballad that is framed with subtle blues guitar that should keep album rock radio interested. Chorus, however, is sweet enough to warrant a push at (the) top forty."

In an interview made for the behind the scenes video of 'Love Conquers All', Ian Paice said; "For the band to play it's very simple. The singer, he can go off and do anything he wants with it because the chord sequence of it is so free, and the singer can actually take it wherever he wants, if he's good enough. You play that with an average singer and he'll just sing it like he heard it on a record. If he's any good, he can go anywhere he wants."

Another strongly melodic track, 'Fortuneteller' is hard despite sounding AOR. It features finger-picked chords from Blackmore. It is a powerful ballad in terms of mood. It is dark and mysterious. So much so that the term "power ballad" probably wouldn't be the best way to describe it on the basis that thematically, the track goes quite a bit further than that.

Jon Lord said; "It's an interesting thing that maybe fifty percent of *Slaves And Masters* has its beginnings in the period from *Perfect Strangers* and onwards. There's one track on it that Ritchie and I had bumping around in our heads since about 1985 called 'Fortuneteller' but it needed Joe to help it. Ian wasn't interested in it but Joe immediately jumped on it. So I think it's a natural progression. It steps outside the line of progression quite obviously by the fact that Joe is singing instead of Ian."

'Too Much Is Not Enough' is a straightforward rocker that picked up the pace. It was written by Turner outside of Deep

Purple, hence the writing credits listing other musicians. In response to why they chose to record a song written by Joe and Al Greenwood, Blackmore said; "When Joe gave me that song to listen to, I liked it from the very beginning. The other guys, too. I have no problem playing other people's songs. A good song is a good song, even if I didn't write it. In fact, to play other people's songs is harder, because you haven't been the composer. It's a huge difference, because I can look at them from another perspective. Some guys in the group think that we should just play our own songs. I think that's wrong. We should play whatever sounds good. As you know, 'Since You Been Gone' and 'I Surrender' were written by someone else, too. Sometimes it's very interesting to play someone else's music. So when it came to 'Too Much Is Not Enough', I was free to choose, and decided to play it, just because I liked it. Many bands only play their own songs. There are situations when someone in the band is presenting everyone an idea and asks the others for their opinion. Sometimes it's very hard to say: 'Sorry, but that's a terrible song.' So you start to say: 'Well, that's not very...', which usually follows the reaction: 'Why? Is the key wrong or do we need to change something else?' Then you have to convince the other guy that it's not possible to use this idea, and gently try to explain him why. Sometimes it happens that musicians start getting at each other's throats because of that... Sometimes I feel like saying: 'What a terrible song.' Instead, you have two to three days of trying to learn it, discussing it with the others and try to convince the person very slowly that this idea doesn't fit into the project. All this just for the sake of avoiding a fight! It takes a lot of effort and nerves. You lose a lot of time in the studio because of that."

As the last track on the album, 'Wicked Ways' brings the full talents of the MkV line-up to the fore. Jon Lord's orchestration brings a tremendous extent of drama to the piece, as does his contribution on keyboards. It sounds like everyone lets loose and gives it their all. At just over six and a half minutes long, the song is a real treat that showcases what MkV are capable of at their best. Blackmore's use of guitar effects is profound but sadly, they are mixed more quietly into the song than say, his use of them in MkII's earlier days (and indeed in Dio era Rainbow) but understandably, if Deep Purple were deliberately going for a more radio friendly sound in 1990, the decisions that may have been made in view of that when it came to mixing are probably ones that made sense at the time.

Blackmore said in November 1990; "You know, sometimes I think it's simply impossible to talk about music. When I'm sitting here at the table I can't give you a serious answer on questions like: 'How do you work on music?' I don't even know what to say to that. But seriously, my favourite song on the album is 'Truth Hurts', which we wrote in five minutes, and I think you can hear that. Joe's voice sounds very good on that one... I also like the song 'Love Conquers All', which is inspired by medieval music, and 'Fire In The Basement', a traditional blues, being played in a shuffle. But we've already talked about it. 'Wicked Ways' is a very versatile song. It has a very unusual descending riff, which we stole from a hit by Loverboy." The song is called 'Working For The Weekend'. When the interviewer relayed this fact to Blackmore, his response: "Oh yeah. That's the song I had in my mind. Of course, it's not a copy, but it was an inspiration for me to write this riff. When I heard it, I thought: 'I'd like to play something in that rhythm'."

Overall, *Slaves And Masters* has a lot going for it in terms of the musical variety it offers. Everyone in MkV brings a lot of talent and writing creativity to the table. It is an imaginative album and the AOR moments certainly are not to the extent that the album feels dumbed down. When promoting the album in interviews, Joe Lynn Turner was keen to assert that people would do well to take it at face value rather than comparing it to Deep Purple's previous work.

It is feasible to consider that *Slaves And Masters* is very ballad based overall. After all, 'King Of Dreams', 'Fortuneteller', 'Truth Hurts' and 'Love Conquers All' make up at least a third of the whole record. But then of course, ballads can be so damn versatile anyway; there is a tremendous difference between say, the average Foreigner track and something with all the character of 'Fortuneteller'. The point being that to write off *Slaves And Masters* as being all about the ballads would be overzealous in view of how versatile Deep Purple are in their ballads on this album.

Slaves And Masters was promoted on television. Music videos were made to promote 'King Of Dreams' and 'Love Conquers All'. 'King Of Dreams' was filmed in Santa Cruz, California. The 'King Of Dreams' video reportedly cost $400,000 to make. When Turner was interviewed for *Kerrang!*, it was put to him that if that was the case, then they had been shafted. "You don't have to tell me that — we had to pay half!" responded Turner. "We brought in Jamie Foley, a film-maker who did *After Dark* and *Who's That Girl?* and it wasn't worth anything. MTV used to be into rock 'n' roll but it's totally oriented towards teenagers now. They don't want to know about us and we didn't believe in tits and ass in videos. Until now. For 'Love Conquers All' we've gone for a bit of surreal tits and ass. It'll work, you mark my words!"

In an interview made for the behind the scenes video of 'Love Conquers All', Joe Lynn Turner said; "It's the quote-unquote power ballad of the record and we felt that it would be a different side of Deep Purple to put out a song like this, as you can hear in the background. Do I like making videos? It's a necessary evil really. We all claim that we don't actually like making them because the hours are long and arduous but at the end of the day I think when we look back and if you have a good one, then it's all worthwhile."

Deep Purple - *Slaves And Masters*: In-depth

Not everyone agreed on how the video for 'Love Conquers All' should have been done. In an interview made for the behind the scenes video, Roger Glover said; "'Love Conquers All' really is a sort of dignified song, it's a song really about love rather than sex, and actually, when it comes to anything, this band is a real problem because we always disagree and there's all sorts of arguments and political cliques and things going on and phone calls across the Atlantic — 'what do you think about this?' — so making a decision is really difficult and the decision on the approach to this video, I was against, and it's got steamy scenes in it but some of the band felt that that's what was needed to get on MTV. Even Sting says this as a matter of fact... That's a terrible one isn't it — the state of affairs becomes ridiculous, that you have to put a girl in your video to get it played. I don't believe in that. I don't like that, and I would much rather have seen the video of us — just a beautifully well-shot performance video. It doesn't have to have all this stuff in it. But unfortunately I was overruled on this, this particular video so it is what it is. I don't particularly like it. I don't think it does anything for the song but then again, as you say, it is steamy and maybe the people that don't have my views will watch it just because it's steamy."

Turner offered his perspective in the same feature: "I see sex selling Cadbury bars. I see sex selling automobiles, anything for that matter."

So, was everyone happy during the recording of *Slaves And Masters*? Well, perhaps not. Upon being asked about his thoughts on the performances from Glover, Paice and Lord on the *Slaves And Masters* album, Blackmore said in November 1990; "It seemed that they were just forcing themselves through it, so they drank a lot of beer."

Jon Lord was quoted in *Keyboard* in January 1994; "When we first came to the studio, the problems piled up and *Slaves And Masters* reflects these problems very well; the musical and personal differences... Roger did some real Herculean work at the time to keep everything together. Sometimes he went to Joe, sometimes to us, always to try and bring us together musically. But it just didn't fit. There was this beautiful piece, which Ritchie and I had written, 'Love Conquers All'. We once played it late at night, that is Ritchie and I played it together. It was very sad, very melancholy, it was introspective, but it was absolutely a Purple song, a bit like 'When A Blind Man Cries' or the quiet parts in 'Child In Time' or 'Wasted Sunsets' — a ballad of the kind we sometimes play, a blues ballad. But then Joe appeared and turned it into some sort of cabaret song... I continuously said: 'No, no, no — what are you doing to the song, what is this gonna be?' The feeling wasn't right from the beginning on. I have really tried to steer the piece into a different direction; I have for example put in a string quartet. I wanted it to sound a little more sour and not so sweet. The term "sweet" could only have been used in a blues context for this piece. It was a sweet little blues, if you know what I mean. But it was not sweet as in "sugary", and Joe sang it like it was a real kitsch ballad!"

In an interview with Japanese radio in 1991, Ian Paice said, "The thing that's different is that Joe has the ability to sing anything well, and because of that it opens up more possibilities than there were before. Ian was a great rock and roll singer, David was a great blues singer, but Joe has the ability to do any and everything, so where there were certain limitations on what we could do before, at the moment anything we can think of he can do, which gives us a lot more. The excitement that can happen on stage becomes more varied because we can do something totally off the wall — sometimes Ritchie will start something, a piece of music that has never existed before, and Joe will sing something, he has the ability to ad lib and be totally spontaneous about it and create a song from nothing. We couldn't do that before, so it just gives us more things to do."

Deep Purple - *Slaves And Masters*: In-depth

Slaves And Masters signified a new era for Deep Purple in terms of the record label it was released on. Blackmore was quoted in *Burrn* in November 1990; "As you know, I love the Germans. BMG is based in West Germany. They work honestly and carefully and co-operating with them is a pleasure. Polydor recently began to use the American methods of doing certain things... Some of my German friends used to work in the headquarters of Polydor, but now they've moved over to BMG. In addition to that, BMG offered us a better contract. But I plan to record a solo album on Polydor, although we haven't reached an agreement on this issue, yet."

Roger Glover's place in Deep Purple certainly seemed solid, as time has shown and rightly so. Blackmore said in *Burrn* in October 1993; "I think that Roger was and still is a very important person in the group. His work, especially in the recording process always helped Deep Purple to function as a group. Today I think that Deep Purple without Roger Glover would be impossible."

Glover was perfect at maintaining a good rapport with everyone. He met up with Gillan after the latter had left the band. There didn't seem to be any animosity between the two. Glover recalled the occurrence in *Metal Hammer* in October 1990; "He gave me a big hug! It didn't feel funny at all as him and me go back a long way. It was our twenty fifth anniversary party (for Episode Six) and it was fantastic. It was great seeing people I hadn't seen for a long time. Some I hadn't seen for twenty-five years and it's interesting to see how people age and you look at yourself to see if you are doing it with dignity. Some of them aren't! We had a photo session with our old photographer and relived those happy moments of pop."

At the Episode Six reunion, they were played some old radio tapes of the band. Glover was quoted "I was struck by how good we were. We had started off as a pure pop band with Beach Boys harmonies then in 1967 we discovered San

Francisco and bands like Love. We moved into the progressive era and the word "heavy" was just coming in. We thought we just had to play the same old stuff — but louder! But that didn't satisfy me very much. We tried really hard but it didn't work and I was disillusioned. But then I heard the first Led Zeppelin album and all I wanted to do was be in a loud heavy blues band."

Upon being asked why Gillan left the band, Glover's response comes across as kind and candid. He told *Metal Hammer* in October 1990; "I haven't worked out a stock reply to that one. It wasn't any one thing. This band is always full of friction, but it was felt the songwriting engine of the band wasn't working. As a band we were playing very well but it wasn't happening on the writing side. It was going nowhere, and I don't know why. Things happen, and change. Nothing stays the same. Something had to change and in the end it was decided Ian should go. It was a joint decision. I love Ian dearly and we'll always be friends and we'll work together again so there was no compunction about meeting each other at the Episode Six reunion. We agreed to talk about anything but we wouldn't talk about Purple! He has a very strong personality and he's not really happy when things aren't the way he wants them. He can work with me because I can compromise. Neither of us is scared to experiment, but as a band Deep Purple *is* scared to experiment because it's a committee and we're watching each other."

There has certainly never been anything boring about Deep Purple when it comes to how they have worked together over the years. In an interview with Japanese radio in 1991, upon being asked his opinion of the rest of Deep Purple, Ian Paice said, "Well, Ritchie is the simplest. A black and white character. It's good or it's bad; I will or I won't. He's there or he's not. There's no middle ground. He's still a terrible practical joker and at times he can drive you crazy, at other times you love him. Jon is a lot more introverted than people think. They see a very polite gentleman, but he tends to keep a lot of his emotions inside. He lets it out through his music. He's a very restrained man. Roger is just a hippie, a leftover hippie. He lives his life for artistic things. Joe, I don't really know that well. He seems to be a party animal, enjoys his life to the full. When it comes to music he's a total professional. Me, you'll have to ask somebody else!"

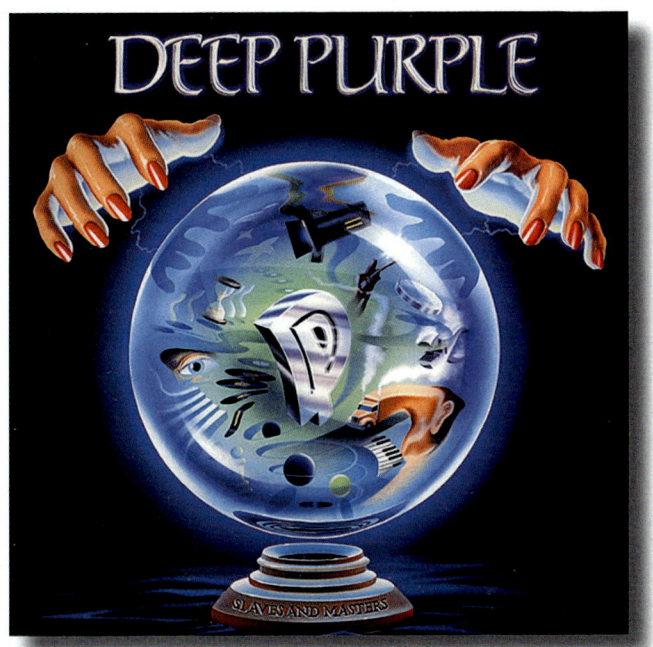

Glover was credited with the art direction for the album. Unlike Deep Purple´s previous studio albums the artwork for Slaves And Masters used various imagery to depict the songs.

Back covers for the LP and CD, showing the different running order.

Argentina

Brazil

Hungary

Whilst there was very little difference in the sleeve designs around the world, there was with the label designs.

USA

Ritchie Blackmore
guitar, winger

Joe Lynn Turner
vocals, midfield

Jon Lord
organ, keyboards, string arrangements

Ian Paice
drums, centre forward

Roger Glover
bass, additional keyboards, defender

Nick Blagona
engineer, goalie

Raymond D'Addario
production assistant, defender

Colin Hart
chief personnel manager, right wing

Charlie Lewis
road manager, goalie

Artie Hoar
road manager, defender

Produced by Roger Glover
Recorded at Greg Rike Productions,
Orlando (Wally Waltman)
Additional recording at
Sountec Studios Inc. (Peter Hodgson),
PowerStation N.Y. (Mathew Lamonica),
Mixed by Nick and Roger at PowerStation N.Y. (Jun Gebert)
Mastered at Sterling Sound (Greg Calbi)

Manager: Bruce Payne, Thames Talent Ltd
Agencies: Premier Talent,
(Frank Barcelona, Barbara Skyder),
The Agency (Neil Warnock),
Technical assistance: NWK (Vince Gutman),
Dreamline (Patty Sprague), Great Sound (Elest)

String orchestra: Jessie Levy
Copying: Joe Marinara Jr.
Travel: Diane Murphy
Cover painting: Thierry Thompson
Art enhancement: Ralph Weems
Art direction: Roger Glover
Photography: Oscar Za

SIDE A

KING OF DREAMS
(Blackmore/Glover/Turner)

It doesn't matter if I'm right or wrong
It really doesn't mean a thing
It doesn't matter if you like my song
As long as you can hear me sing
'Cause I'm the thorn in every little girl's nose
You know I cut but never bleed
A shadow in the night, pure delight
I can satisfy your every need

Don't make a difference what you got
It doesn't matter what you lose
Don't make a difference if you like it or not
Baby I'm gonna change your attitude
'Cause all around me there is mystery and wonder
You can't you see it in my eyes
I'll crack the sky, make you feel the thunder
You'll never see through my disguise

I'm a real smooth dancer, I'm a fantasy man
Master of illusion, magic touch in my hand
All the stages are empty when I steal the scenes
A beggar of love, second hand hero ... King of Dreams

All around, all around
Emotional squeeze through again and again
I know how to please you, your mind is on the bend
Can't you feel the power, surrender in my arms
Beyond the witching hour we're travelling on and on

I'm a real smooth dancer, I'm a fantasy man
Master of illusion, magic touch in my hands
The stages are empty when I steal the scenes
A beggar of love, second hand hero ... King of Dreams

I'm a real smooth dancer, fantasy man
Master of illusion, sleight of hand
The stages are empty when I steal the scenes
A beggar for love ... King of Dreams

THE CUT RUNS DEEP
(Blackmore/Glover/Turner/Lord/Paice)

Got your finger on the trigger
Your cold eyes taking aim
You took a shot at my heart
Let the bullets fly
Tell me has one of them got my name

What about the hearts he
What about the emptiness inside
It doesn't just fade away
Turning the knife
How much can I bleed
The cut runs deep

I can't find no salvation
Can't find no healing touch
Reaching out for mercy
A stranger in your eyes
I want you too much

What about the hearts he
What about the emptiness inside
It doesn't just fade away
Turning the knife
How much can I bleed
The cut runs deep

FIRE IN THE BASEMENT
(Blackmore/Glover/Turner/Lord/Paice)

I came bound to your front door, your back door was locked
Pushed your button, rang your bell, you didn't hear me knock
I saw your window open wide, so I crawled inside
Ran to the top floor, but you were on the ground
I was on my way up and you were going down

Fire in the basement
Burn me up, scream and shout
Fire in the basement
Only you can put it out

This strange sensation that I'm going through
Sweet infatuation when I get next to you
I know what it takes to be a man, you understand
'Cause when the sparks start flying you'll never be the same
Then it'll be too late to leave you girl but I'm so glad I came

Fire in the basement
Burn me up, scream and shout
Fire in the basement
Only you can put it out

Smoky eyes burning bright
Innocence lost, satisfy my appetite
Surrender to the Faster, what's your name
Let's get down to business, how can you refuse
Give this baby a helping hand, come on light my fuse

FORTUNETELLER
(Blackmore/Glover/Turner/Lord/Paice)

Cast your eyes into the crystal
Deep inside the mystery
Is that a vision of a lonely man
I fear it looks a lot like me

Is that a man without a woman
Whose empty life is but a shell
Empty hearts will echo
Forever in the wishing well

Fortuneteller
You've got to help me find an end to the nightmare
'Cause I can't stand this pain and the curse of time
Somewhere in your eyes I'll find the answer
Give me the truth I've been looking for
By my guiding light, I'll take my chances
Turn the card, seal my fate, close the door

Some days come with a vengeance
Some days I feel so bad
The mirror holds no secrets
I feel the best thing that I had

Fortuneteller
Can you help me to see, is there an end to the sorrow
Or was this slow ride to nowhere always meant to be
Somewhere in your eyes I'll find the answer
Give me the truth I've been looking for
By my guiding light, I'll take my chances
Turn the card, seal my fate, close the door

She was always taking more than she'd need
But we were both to blame somehow
In the heat of the moment I told her to leave
I guess I had more than I found
But I remember ...

SIDE B

TRUTH HURTS
(Blackmore/Glover/Turner)

You know my will is broken
You've got my heart on hold
I'm living here in pieces, so cold
It gets so hard to handle
All the things you need to say
But I guess I heard it all before anyway
Is love such a blessing or a curse
Either way
Truth hurts

Well there'll be no more running
Now I've got you face to face
I want to know who you've been losing to my place
You say I had it coming
Try to hold my head up high
Love gave me wings and left me paralyzed

There's nothing left alive
As we watch the spirits die
The world keeps turning
My heart keeps learning
Do you know where the guilty sleep

Babe I've got my pride
Somehow I will survive
The world keeps turning
My heart keeps learning
Do you know where the lonely sleep tonight

Another fallen angel
How far I just can't tell
Living without love is a living hell
Why in love such is a blessing or a curse
Baby either way
Truth hurts

Baby I've got my pride
Somehow I will survive
My heart keeps learning
Don't know which is worse
But one thing that I know
Truth hurts

LOVE CONQUERS ALL
(Blackmore/Glover/Turner)

Feels like the end
When you're closer to losing your dreams
Than losing a friend
Flying blind
I'm shooting in the dark
Who am I foot
Oh girl
And if it takes me a lifetime
I swear I'll tear down every wall
Love conquers all

Oh my way
Tomorrow I rise with the sun
Soon I'll be gone
Words can't say
How the memories of feelings of love
They linger on
Oh girl
And if it takes me forever
I know it's a worth every teardrop that falls
Love conquers all

Somewhere there's a place in your heart
Where the sounds never heal
Well you're not alone
That's just how I feel

Love conquers all
This one will last a lifetime
And if love conquers all,
This one will last forever

BREAKFAST IN BED
(Blackmore/Glover/Turner)

Woke up this morning, rain coming down
Washing the sin from the street
Sometimes I feel like I'm being ground
Just trying to make ends meet
Well I work every day to sweat out my dreams
Won't you show me that you understand
It's only my life, whatever that means
And you've put it all in your hands

I need someone to pull me through
Won't you take the pain from my head
Give me all your loving the way you always do
Give me breakfast in bed

I feel like the good days are numbered
And my nights are getting too long
My hopes and my fears take their toll on the years
And my will power's almost gone
Well it's a time full of trouble
A time of desperate need
Sometimes life don't make sense
Fighting the anger, jealousy and greed
One day I'll look back and wonder where it all went

I need someone to pull me through
Won't you take the pain from my head
Give me all your loving, the way you always do
Give me breakfast in bed

It don't take much to please me
I'm just a simple man
Won't you please believe me
I gotta tell you
It don't take much—a tender touch
So baby do the best that you can

TOO MUCH IS NOT ENOUGH
(Turner/Held/Greenwood)

You're so extreme, you're so super heavy
You're one step over the line
Not what you seem, don't try and tell me
I know what's really on your mind

Once you got started you're out of control
Don't play that sweet and innocent with me girl
I know you know you want to rock and roll
But I got just what you need

I, I want to feel your love
Too much is not enough
I, I want to feel your touch
Too much is not enough

You've got it bad, you're so hopelessly addicted
You're always searching for the cure
Love is the crime, you stand convicted
You keep on coming back for more

Come on admit it, you're over the top
That song and dance won't work with me girl
You just can't quit it, don't know when to stop
But I got the remedy

I, I want to feel your love
Too much is not enough
I, I want to feel your touch
Too much is not enough

Baby stop wasting time
And let me know that you're mine
I need to feel your embrace
How much can I take

WICKED WAYS
(Blackmore/Glover/Turner/Lord/Paice)

You're so hot, you're so cool
I can see that you're nobody's fool
Now tell me am I coming through
It's too late, I can't wait
Believe it's gonna be a big mistake
But I'm tempted to believe in you

I don't want to run and I don't want to fight
I just want to be the one you love tonight
Unclose my eyes, let it be

Bring on the band of angels from the great divide
I'll never get to heaven so take me for a ride
Fruit on the tree is shaking, my mind is in a daze
Just want a taste of your love
And learn your wicked ways

You're so bad, it feels good
There's so much I never understood
Oh Mama take a look at me now
I'm hung up, strung out
All I want to do is scream and shout your name
Addicted to you somehow

Electric is your touch there's magic in your kiss
You know I never knew that love could feel like this
Unclose my eyes, set me free

Bring on the band of angels from the great divide
I'll never get to heaven so take me for a ride
Fruit on the tree is shaking, my mind is in a daze
Just want a taste of your love
And learn your wicked ways

All songs published by Blackmore's Music Ltd., Rugged Music Ltd.,
and Administered by Thames Overtures Ltd. except 'Too Much is
Not Enough' published by EMI Screen Gems.

Thanks to: Rudi Gassner, Hans Herm, Michael Dornemann,
Greg Rike, Danie Rice, Barbara Fucigna, Mark Wexler,
Melissa Dreger, Nancy Scricca, Ben Kaye, Susan Miles,
Michelle Deleu, Ed Goldsery, Billy Squier, Brian O'Shea,
Brittiton MacHan, Joe Mardox

© 1990 BMG Music ℗ 1990 BMG Music

The major sleeve variant occurred in Australia. Whereas everywhere else the album was released in a single sleeve with an inner sleeve, the Australians used the inner sleeve to make it a gatefold album.

Greece

Peru

A couple of cassette variations.

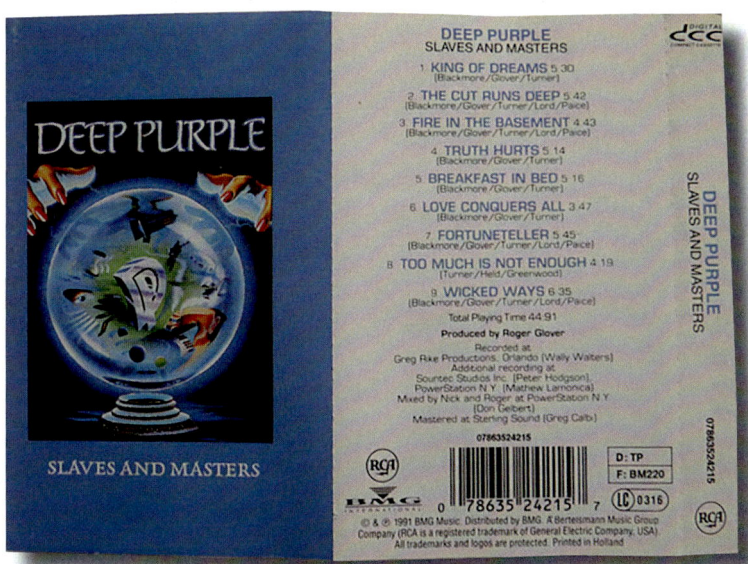

The album was also released on the short-lived digital compact cassette format.

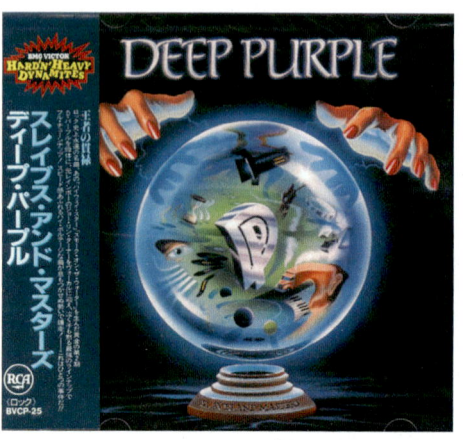
Original CD

1999 reissue

2006 reissue

2008 reissue

It was the first Deep Purple album not to be released in Japan on vinyl. However the 2006 reissue was a CD size paper sleeve replica of the vinyl sleeve, complete with the inner sleeve.

Deep Purple - *Slaves And Masters*: In-depth

Chapter Three
Touring

Turner told *Metal Hammer* in October 1990; "The aim for me is to bring fire to the stage. I just hope audiences have an open mind and don't think about Gillan or even Coverdale being in the band. Hell, there have been so many Purples. Why not this one?"

As has been the case throughout much of Deep Purple's history, it was considered that playing live would be an excellent opportunity to expand upon the ideas that featured on the studio album and when it came to *Slaves And Masters*, that philosophy was no different. In an interview with Japanese radio in 1991, Ian Paice said, "I think it's much more difficult now to get someone to listen to eight, nine or ten minutes of one piece of music, so this is a time when songs are much more important. What we try and do is to get as much into the song as we can on the record and accept that that's it for the album. When we take that to the stage then it can be as it was, you can extend it, have fun, put a long solo in it, but records are a different thing now. It was a lot freer fifteen to twenty years ago. What is acceptable to record companies and radio is a lot more closely defined."

In the run up to the tour, much was said in the music press about the absence of Ian Gillan. It was considered in the *Asbury Park Press* November 1990; "The latest chapter in the saga of Deep Purple is a bitter sweet one. The sweet part: a new album (*Slaves And Masters*), is to be followed by a tour, which kicks off in January. The bitter part: singer Ian Gillan has been kicked out of what the rock press calls Purple's "MkII" (or "*Machine Head*") line-up... This happened before, in 1974 (sic — it happened in 1973!) But back then, Glover was also a casualty in the revolution. This time, he's survived the cut. A press release blamed the catch-all "creative differences" for the split."

Glover was quoted in the same feature; "It's very difficult to actually put it in a nutshell, and I don't really like talking about it, because, to me, it's still a painful thing to go through. Ian has been a good friend of mine and he's still a good friend of mine. We're still in contact. We still talk. It got to a point where it became an only way out. I can't put it any other way. I can't give you concrete reasons. And I don't really want to talk about it."

Joe Lynn Turner spoke to *Kerrang!* in March 1991; "All I really care about is that the live thing is turning me on one hundred percent. We're more hard rockin' now. Gillan's voice is brilliant, but I've got a nastier rock voice when I want it... We're having a lot of fun on stage and the shows are getting better every night. All that "mates" stuff — it's usually a load of shit. I don't think many groups are genuine. There's a lot of chequebook rock 'n' roll about and I don't mind admitting that we see enough of each other on tour. I don't wanna hang out. All I'm bothered about is a great gig."

Importantly, there was no animosity between Turner and Gillan. Turner told the *Asbury Park Press* November 1990; "I have met Ian Gillan only briefly and only once at Irvine, in California, but he got a message down to me through Roger, who he's excellent friends with. It said: 'Congratulations. Good luck. Sing as you sing. You're a great vocalist. All the best.' And I just thought that was the warmest, most gentleman-like thing he could do."

Also, in an interview made for the behind the scenes video of 'Love Conquers All', Turner said; "As far as Ian Gillan and replacing him, I'm so used to replacing people that it's getting really boring and old right now. But I have one philosophy — people say that it's big shoes to fill, it's just that I don't think I'm filling any shoes, I just think I'm making new footprints. I do it my way, you know, and I do what I have to do. I sing the old classics my way without losing the song content and he was very kind to me Ian, he said 'you're a great singer in your own right and you have great talent so don't let anybody give you the bullets. You know, just go on and do what you have to do. Make yourself proud.' And I appreciated that."

It was asserted in *Metal Hammer* in October 1990; "Before Deep Purple fans start complaining that Joe Lynn Turner should not be following in the mighty Ian Gillan's shoes, they should be aware of Joe's background. As well as singing with Ritchie in Rainbow, he actually started out his career singing Deep Purple songs in a cover band called Ezra."

To which Turner added, "It was a very heavy band. We played all the songs they did. They had a recording contract but we didn't! So I'm comfortable with the Purple sound. A, They are my favourite band and B, I grew up on them. So with this album we tried to bring back the roots, and when we get on stage we'll play a lot of the old stuff which will be pretty good fun! Mind you, Ritchie gets awfully moody sometimes and he'll say 'I don't wanna play that shit!' but it's my contention that the audience should get what they pay for. We should give them their money's worth."

By this stage in their careers, Deep Purple were seasoned professionals who knew what they were about. It was very much a case of "what you see is what you get."

Blackmore told *Burrn* in November 1990; "Perhaps most musicians start to play music from an interior anxiety and self-doubt, and the music becomes some sort of determination for them. We feel calmer and more stable, holding a musical instrument in our hands and playing music. I'm not one of those who radiates self-confidence, and I've also never felt quite fulfilled. Maybe the lack of self-confidence attracts so many people about me?... My friends are often surprised when they see that I don't want to talk about my music. People ask me why, but I don't want to discuss it with pride. And on stage, when I play the guitar, I'm the centre of attention, and, in fact, for me it's easier to do this than working as a carpenter, when no one is seeing me. I can't imagine myself doing this! I could never work as a carpenter just for the sake of making money."

In response to the comment of "With the instrumental fire power behind him, was Joe at all concerned that they might blow him away on stage," Turner said to *Metal Hammer* in October 1990; "It could get out of hand, but if Malmsteen didn't swamp me, this band won't. But Ritchie's not like that. He's the most selfless person, when it comes to writing. He always makes sure the singer is up front and the guitar is well placed. Whereas with Yngwie it was 'make the guitar loud and fuck the singer.' Ritchie is a song man. He knows how to express himself on guitar without blowing too much. He's a real pro. When we did this record, he said 'Thank God. I've always wanted a singer. We'd play these tracks and Gillan would just yell over them.' He feels this album is more like *Machine Head*."

There are two separate occasions that could be regarded as Joe Lynn Turner's stage debut with Deep Purple. Officially, MkV first performed at the Palác Kultury a Sportu in Ostrava, Czechoslovakia at the beginning of the *Slaves And Masters* tour on 4th February 1991. The gig was met with a lot of media attention, so much so that it was recorded for Czech television.

Unofficially though, Turner's stage debut with Deep Purple was in December 1989 where he performed with just Blackmore, Glover and Paice at the Red Fox Inn in Vinhall, Vermont. The purpose of the gig was to have a jam in front of an audience. It was a casual affair to the extent that nobody minded that Jon Lord didn't take part. Colin Hart recalled in his autobiography; "To celebrate (Turner's recruitment) we did a gig in the local pub, the Red Fox Inn, but without Jon Lord who declined to play in such cramped surroundings. It was just to let off steam really, so nobody minded him being absent."

Turner was the first non-British vocalist (and to this day is the only non-British vocalist) to be welcomed into the band. All other American members of the group have been guitarists (Tommy Bolin, Joe Satriani, and Steve Morse).

Despite the apprehensions of some, there was a lot of belief in the album and in the new line-up prior to the start of the tour. Many fans weren't very happy about Joe Lynn Turner being in the band. Blackmore responded to this in *Burrn* in November 1990; "People who hate listening to this album should forget about the old Deep Purple for a moment. I think that *Slaves And Masters* is a new era for the band. When we decided to change the vocalist, we'd heard a lot of other singers before Joe. But they didn't have the character, which Joe's voice has. We were not sure whether we should choose Joe, due to the fact that he sang in Rainbow, and we would be three old members of Rainbow, which is why we were afraid of using Joe. But well, I think you should listen to the album to decide whether you like it or not. I like Joe and think that he did an excellent job. I believe that you have to listen to the albums yourself. I hate when people just listen to some people telling them that it's rubbish. I like this album very much personally."

With the tour having started in Czechoslovakia, it carried on across Europe and Scandinavia before a seven-date UK leg that took place between 10th and 17th March with Vixen as support. It included four sold out nights at Hammersmith Odeon. With a month's break thereafter, the tour then carried on to the US. Colin Hart recalled; "The tour headed to America (to) start in Burlington, Vermont, but it would only run for eight shows, a sure indication that the public just wasn't accepting Joe or that it had had it with Deep Purple. The shows were confined to the East Coast with the only stand out date being at Radio City Music Hall in Manhattan."

Hart's theories are debateable. It could have been down to the fans not accepting Joe Lynn Turner or it could have been because people weren't interested in Deep Purple anymore by that point. It's all very subjective and there's no real way of being able to tell what the main factors were. It was probably a bit of both. However, in 1990 and 1991, information wasn't as widely available then as it is now; the fact is that if the music press were failing (or indeed declining) to advertise the fact that Deep Purple were touring, there is a likelihood that there are plenty of fans who would have happily gone to see the show, had they been aware of it! I say this on the basis that when Blackmore reformed Rainbow for his 1995 album, *Stranger In Us All*, I know of several fans who said they would have loved to have seen a show or two but simply missed out because they weren't even aware that a tour was happening in the first place!

That's the nineties for you; there was such a diversity of interesting music being put forward by artists who had been working on their craft for decades but if they weren't new/funky/fresh — or whatever the media wanted to call them at the time — it is plausible that they were underrepresented in the media to the extent that essentially, the fans missed them (bearing in mind that hardcore fans and casual fans probably engage differently on how they follow a musician's career but nevertheless, would probably be up for seeing them live).

Next, it was on to Japan, Thailand and then Singapore. It was then on to Brazil before going back to Europe and then finishing in Israel on the 29th September 1991.

With a new vocalist as frontman, it was agreed by everyone that it was a good time to renew the setlist. Glover told *Metal Hammer* in October 1990; "There is plenty of room for stage performances on a lot of these tracks. That's good because on *The House Of Blue Light* none of them worked live. It's a problem that has plagued the band since time immemorial. The last album we did that had a bunch of stuff that turned into good live songs was *Machine Head*. Hardly any of the songs on *Who Do We Think We Are* made it live. *Perfect Strangers* yielded only two numbers and *The House Of Blue Light* yielded none that worked live. We have been doing the basic *Machine Head* set for so long it's become a yawn. There is a different feeling in the band now and this one will spawn a lot more and the stage act is gonna change considerably."

The new setlist resulted in 'Burn' being used as the opening song. Jon Lord said to *Kerrang!* in March 1991; "As for the old material, we've always started off with 'Highway Star' but I think we'll try and start with something different this time. Surely audiences are sophisticated enough — even those who come along to hear 'Smoke On The Water' only — surely their imaginations are wide-ranging enough to accept some new stuff. I'm sure they are. One suggestion I made for Joe — and the other guys seem to have agreed — was for him to take away everything we've done and choose a handful of songs for himself, that he wouldn't mind doing."

Most of the songs from *Slaves And Masters* were used as part of the set and fan favourites were kept in place. As a result, a typical set for the *Slaves And Masters* tour went something like this:

Burn
Black Night
~ occasionally including a small segment of Long Live Rock 'n' Roll
Truth Hurts
The Cut Runs Deep
~ usually including Hush and very occasionally, Child In Time
Perfect Strangers

Fire In The Basement
~ *bass solo*
King Of Dreams
Love Conquers All (with Joe Lynn Turner on acoustic guitar)
Difficult To Cure
~ *keyboard solo*
Knocking At Your Back Door
Lazy
Highway Star
Smoke On The Water
~ *drum solo and Woman From Tokyo*

For the 1991 tour, Deep Purple were even open to dropping the drum solo. Jon Lord told *Kerrang!* in March 1991; "I think a drum solo would only be necessary if Ian Paice wanted to do one. If he doesn't want to do one then I'm quite happy not to have one, although it does provide us with a good opportunity to go off for a pee!"

At some of the earlier shows, 'Wicked Ways' was sometimes played after 'Lazy'. It was only at the last show that 'Space Truckin'' was played. Very small segments of 'Fortuneteller' were included in some shows but the song was never performed in full. For the US leg of the tour, 'King Of Dreams' was dropped from the setlist but it was used as an encore in Japan. Some shows sporadically included covers of the following songs: 'Tutti Frutti', 'Yesterday', 'A Whiter Shade Of Pale', 'Stand By Me' and 'Hey Joe'.

Not all of the songs that were rehearsed made it into the setlist. Joe Lynn Turner stated in some interviews that 'Too Much Is Not Enough' and even 'Fireball' were considered for performance. In an interview with *Rockline Radio*, he also said that he would be interested in performing 'Pictures Of Home'. Whilst the song never got an airing as part of the Deep Purple

MkV live set, Turner later went on to perform the track on Yngwie Malmsteen's 1996 album, *Inspiration*.

In interviews long after MkV was no more, Jon Lord revealed that Joe was told to choose songs that he wanted to do and that he was encouraged to pick from Deep Purple's entire discography. Equally though, Blackmore has asserted in a number of interviews that he had more say than Turner in what could be performed from the back catalogue. Between them, Blackmore and Turner wanted to do several Rainbow numbers. Years later, Blackmore stated that it may have been possible to persuade Jon Lord on the matter but that Ian Paice was in absolute refusal.

It's exciting to think that with Turner in the band, it became possible to have 'Burn' in the setlist. With it originally being a Coverdale and Hughes era track, it had not had an airing for some time on stage. The MkV setlist was immensely far removed from the *Made In Japan* type setlist that MkII had stuck with since reforming in 1984. Due to bootlegging, it is possible to hear the ways in which Deep Purple MkV evolved as a live ensemble. Further to this, it is fortunate that both their first and last official shows of the 1991 tour were recorded for TV and radio. As a result, it is possible to look back on this period of the band's history with a broad perspective (on the bootleg-sourcing front, the material is out there if you're willing to dig for it).

The 1991 tour made use of what was a revolutionary laser lighting system at the time. Jon Lord explained to *Kerrang!* in March 1991; "It's fed through fibre optics up into a moving light. It goes into a prismatic lens at the end of the lights so you can alter the laser beam in a myriad of different ways — split it and change it and do all sorts of things with it. We have eight of those suspended from the truss above the stage and we can do the most remarkable things with them. We've got them exclusively until the end of the world tour."

Musically, the MkV live shows had a lot going for them. Of course they're a very different animal to gigs like Stuttgart 1993 as part of *The Battle Rages On...* tour. But that's okay. With MkV, Blackmore's playing sounds a lot freer and more relaxed than it perhaps does on recordings of live shows from 1987 and 1988. Of course, that's quite a broad statement to make on my part but genuinely — if you haven't already — I strongly urge you to have a comparative listen in such regard.

Joe Lynn Turner said to *Kerrang!*; "I like a challenge. I don't follow in anybody else's footsteps, I make my own. I'm not lickin' anyone's ass. It's not about how much you drank, who you fucked and how many guitar strings you can stick up your ass — although I can get twelve up mine! It's about the music! The bottom line is that I'm here to do the best job I can for Deep Purple. I love the past and I'm excited about the future. Damn the torpedoes, and the slings and arrows of outrageous fortune. In other words, fuck 'em!"

Regardless of where people may feel Joe Lynn Turner does (or indeed doesn't) sit as a member of Deep Purple, the fact is that he did an excellent job in his performance of the songs he wrote when touring them in 1991. As for the Deep Purple songs written by others, well, Turner had some big shoes to fill and it is understandable as to why the jury was very much out on that one at the time. But as a seasoned professional, did he give it his all when he stepped up to the mic? Well, many still think so and long live the bootleg recordings that now give everyone the chance to make up their own minds. The trouble with bootlegs of course is that they're not officially catalogued. Due to this, when writing about them, I'm always cautious to add that the version I've heard might be different to the version that others heard; the quality might be different and even the content and quirky names by which the bootlegs go by might be different too. Essentially it's an unregulated field. I'm going to offer some commentary on what are some recordings of significance but for further listening, it is definitely worth exploring such recordings outside of this book.

In terms of the value of bootlegs, as Roger Glover was quoted in *Goldmine* in July 2011; "I could never understand our success; I could never understand why so many people bought our records, because they were so full of flaws! And then I started listening to bootlegs and to what we really were, and I came to reassess the whole thing. Listening to bootlegs from the early seventies, I realised what a dangerous band we were, and how exciting it was not to know what was going to happen next. We walked a very thin line between chaos and order, and that was the magic, that was why people bought our records. I came from a pop band (Episode Six), and when you're a pop band, you learn the song, and you play it the same way every night. And now, there's this band veering off, and suddenly the solo's in E when it should be... 'hey, what's happening here?' — that's the magic."

December 1989, Red Fox Inn, Vinhall, Vermont:
The show performed by just Turner, Blackmore, Glover and Paice. In the background, members of the audience can be heard discussing who's on stage and it turns out that some of them aren't sure who's who. It is very much a warm-up in the sense that so much tuning is done that Turner eventually placates the audience by telling them that the band is "tuning because we care".

Blackmore's guitar is very loud compared to the other musicians but considering the small size of the venue and the fact that the gig was more about fun than a commercial effort, it's a pleasure to listen to. Lord's absence is such that Blackmore has to work harder to deliver on the melody front; his playing sounds incredibly enthusiastic and there is a sense that morale is good, particularly in comparison to his live playing in 1988. As well as 'Smoke On The Water', the newly acquainted MkV cover 'Going Down' and 'That'll Be The Day'.

6th February 1991, Zagreb Dom Sportova, Croatia:
It is evident that it had been a while since 'Burn' was on the setlist — it takes Blackmore quite a few rounds of the riff to get into it rhythmically. An interesting insight into MkV in the early stages of touring.

17th February 1991, Sporthalle, Hamburg, Germany:
This bootleg goes by the name of *Ritchie Laughs*. When Turner sings the first verse of 'Smoke On The Water', it sounds almost like he is doing a theme and variation version of the song due to how melodically he plays on the lyrics melismatically. The sound quality of the bootleg that I listened to peaks and dips quite a bit but with bootlegs being what they are, your mileage may vary. Nevertheless, an interesting insight into the interesting quirks that Turner brought to the band.

6th March 1991, Forum, Copenhagen, Denmark /
16th March 1991, Hammersmith Odeon, London:
This bootleg goes by the name of *A Whiter Shade Of Purple*, probably named as such due to the fact that it includes Deep Purple covering the Procol Harum song, 'A Whiter Shade Of Pale'. This is one of three tracks on this bootleg from London, that were added to the complete show from Copenhagen. A worthwhile bootleg to own, also for the entertaining moment of hearing Jon Lord speak to the crowd between songs — also from the London part of this release.

10th April 1991, Burlington Memorial Hall, Vermont:
The first date from the US leg of the *Slaves And Masters* tour. It is clear that this bootleg is labelled correctly because Joe Lynn Turner mentions the location when addressing the audience. 'Fire In The Basement' is played with more

energy and aggression than it is on the album. 'Difficult To Cure' is on point; it sounds tremendously accurate and highly enthusiastic, as does 'Knocking At Your Back Door'. A fantastic improvisation moment takes place when Jon Lord plays a small segment of 'In The Hall Of The Mountain King' and the rest of the band joins in. A magical moment and something that was very underplayed (if at all mentioned) in the reviews of the live shows at the time.

22nd April 1991, Pittsburgh Syria Mosque, Pennsylvania:
The audience sound up for this gig and then some. So much so that the sound quality on this bootleg is impaired. It doesn't matter though. It is clear that musically Deep Purple are on top form and once again Turner confirms the venue of the gig when talking to the audience. During 'Truth Hurts', a few lines from 'Fortuneteller' are cleverly weaved in. 'Love Conquers All' is performed with heart and soul. Lord's solo during 'Knocking At Your Back Door' evokes a rousing cheer from the audience. It sounds like Turner is struggling vocally somewhat on 'Highway Star' but on balance, it is played a lot faster than it had been done in the MkII live gigs. In the same regard, 'Lazy' is played significantly faster on this one too.

It was reported in *Kerrang!* in March 1991; "If you were to believe every cynic in town, the Purple are dead and awaiting burial, and the stink of the corpse is all but overpowering. So could someone explain to me exactly why the Sporthalle in Hamburg is packed to the rafters with a health amalgam of young and old cognoscenti this evening, and exactly why I'm sitting up in the Gods scribbling liberally and wearing out the nib of my pencil when I stab at exclamation marks following words such as 'dynamic', 'tasteful', 'tremendous' and 'balls out'?"

"Is this the same hoary old dinosaur on stage that everyone

is telling me is the laughing stock of rock? Don't think so, suckers. Surely some mistake? I don't care how unhip I am. Deep Purple were the fuckin' business here tonight! From the moment the lights went down, the lasers went up and the crowd went apeshit, this was an event par excellence. Not a wayward trip down memory lane. Not a disgraceful continuation of a long-gone legend either, but actually a totally bona fide rock 'n' roll band, with or without wigs, performing their craft with consummate professionalism and convincing heart."

"Okay, so there was none of this Hi-NRG, all-action performance that you might expect from the younger puppies, but that was never what Purple were about anyhow. What we got was a valid rock 'n' roll musical statement, without the circus theatrics, which brought things into perspective. Granted, Joe Lynn Turner's leather pants were ludicrously tight, but come on, what are we talking about here — a fashion show or music? I would just as soon have been spared four guys in their forties prancing about around the stage like they had burning coals in their pants anyway. Come and tell me that opening a show with 'Burn' or giving us a stonking version of 'Highway Star' is bogus and I'll call you all of ignorant, naïve and cloth-eared!"

"The new material from the totally excellent and vastly underrated *Slaves And Masters* album was both performed and greeted with obvious relish from both sides. There's a whole lot of new material served up with spice, 'The Cut Runs Deep' and 'Truth Hurts' in particular dragging every ounce of splendour from the musos. When the show, complemented by a cleverly devised laser display, manages to move you as much as this, then all the controversy, all the back-stabbing and shit-stirring, makes not a jot of difference."

I love this report. Why? Because it starts off in a way that smacks of, "oh, here we go, the kool *Kerrang!* journalist isn't going to give Deep Purple a fair hearing because he introduces them by going to great lengths to insinuate that the band is morbidly old."

From the opening of the report, it really comes across that the journalist is going to be embarrassingly derogatory towards a great band on the basis of their ages alone. But no, the report evolves to compliment Deep Purple on everything that they got right on the night as true professionals with a wealth of enjoyable new material presented with innovation and emotion. Looking at the review overall, the beginning could be regarded as misleading and even, somewhat offensive. On the other hand though, perhaps it's a kase of kudos to the *Kerrang!* journalist for being candid in refusing to deny or gloss over how some fans may have viewed Deep Purple as they presented in 1991. By presenting a balanced backdrop of the doubts that many may have held about the band, it does, in fairness, exemplify the fact that they put on a damn good show — not in denial of the doubters but in spite of them.

It was reported in a Brazilian newspaper in 1991; "The old rock bands — "dinosaurs" — as they are called, seem to be destined to become new Glenn Miller orchestras (or Ray Conniff, if you prefer). Every year they come back with new formations and old songs to pack the peripheral stages of the planet. They're artists who live off the name. No, it's not about brontosaurus Bob Dylan, who sang in the city on Friday and Saturday, but Deep Purple, the group that had their days of glory in the early seventies. The Purple (who has played Friday and Saturday in the stadium of Ibirapuera) presents today at the Olympia, with a young singer, a certain Joe Lynn Turner, who with a few screamings in the style Robert Plant manages to assassinate the old classics of the band while Ritchie Blackmore, Roger Glover, Jon Lord and Ian Paice try to regain the vigour of twenty years past, even if it is necessary to wear leather clothes."

"They attack Beethoven's 9th Symphony with zeal. The public almost packed the gym of Ibirapuera on Friday and

Deep Purple - *Slaves And Masters*: In-depth

Saturday nights to worship their idols. Formed by old grey-haired hippies and long-haired young headbangers, the two held on for a two-and-a-half hour delay on Friday, and an hour on Saturday, to re-live old hits like 'Hush', 'Child In Time', 'Highway Star', 'Lazy' and 'Smoke On The Water', among others, and endure some new heavy ballads worthy of FM radio. But the truth is that this glorious band no longer has the impetus of yore, barely even managing to get through the rhythm in some songs ('Lazy' was regrettable). And, to make matters worse, Jon Lord still played Chopin and Gershwin. But it doesn't matter — after all, another "living legend" was here. And Ritchie Blackmore (who, they say, is a better football player than guitarist) still broke his guitar on Saturday, in a ritual sacrifice long-forgotten (which reminded me of the film *Top Secret — Superconfidential*, when Val Kilmer sings in a restaurant and a very old musician shreds his guitar against the amplifier). The audience liked it and applauded. Well, if it's just rock and roll, who doesn't?"

A very mixed review indeed! An overall feel of, "It was nice to see them because they're Deep Purple and they're clearly living off the name: Some bits were worthy but others were pitiful." It's certainly a balanced review in the sense that because the reviewer stated what they didn't like, it adds validity to the bits they highlighted as being good. Hmm, it's so subjective though really. Difficult to comment perhaps? What the review does show though is that no matter what Deep Purple MkV did or didn't do on stage, there was always going to be that inevitable level of expectation working against them based on their legacy and previous output. It's certainly endearing that the gig attracted audiences across the age spectrum (dinosaurs indeed!). Notably, it seems that Deep Purple were certainly welcome in Brazil in 1991; they played seven dates there as part of the *Slaves And Masters* tour.

It is an unavoidable fact that for many Deep Purple fans at

the time, the question of "where's Gillan?" would have been an overriding theme of the *Slaves And Masters* tour. It is plausibly an unpleasant experience for anyone to be giving it their all on stage only to be dismissed on the basis that they're not "the other guy". It must have been exasperating at times. Joe Lynn Turner was quoted in *Kerrang!* in March 1991; "I don't know what the fuck they (the fans) want! I think they just want to live in the past. A lot of them are nostalgic fools who don't realise that today is 1991, but in many ways we opened the door to that, no question about it."

In one particular interview, Turner had a moment of coming across as somewhat bitter about the whole thing but hey, it is what it is: "The sad thing is that most people don't seem to have any interest in the music now, even if you've released a surprisingly great album. They're more interested in whether you wear a wig! Fuck all that shit! What does it *sound* like? If you don't like it, fine, but what has any of the rest of it got to do with anything? Most music mags are worse than *National Enquirer*! If I was a pop star, all the other stuff would be relevant, but I'm not! At the end of the day, all I really care about is that they spell my name right! I'm in Deep Purple, I'm singing well, I'm writing great songs and quite frankly, you can kiss my fuckin' ass! All that other stuff sounds like sour grapes to me. If you have to bitch with me then we'll go into a room and slam around. One on one. Let's go! See whose dick is longer! Who cares what the magazines say about me? The women don't! That's another music biz story, that I'm a puff. Let me tell you, I've fucked more women that they've ever seen — and *I'm* a puff! Back in '81 in Rainbow I used to get wound up by this stuff, but Ritchie said if you're gonna believe the good stuff, then you've got to believe the bad stuff, so don't believe any fuckin' thing!... As far as I'm concerned, if *Rolling Stone* hate the LP then we must be doing something right! If Mick Box from Uriah Heep thinks 'Love Conquers All' sounds like a weak Foreigner, then we must be doing something right, 'cause what's he done? Let the kids decide. I'm for the kids who pay good, hard money to come to the shows, who grew up on the street like I did. Enough of these fuckin' bollocks bastards who sit back and point the finger!"

In all fairness, Deep Purple MkV had quite a lot going against them commercially. It was twofold; they didn't fit the mould of nineties hard rock and they weren't, to the frustration of many fans, MkII. In such regard, if Turner was having a bit of a moan in that interview, fair play really. Colin Hart stated; "The tour was going okay despite a less than enthusiastic reaction to the album, but calls for Gillan could be heard in those little quiet interludes in the show. Annoying, especially for Joe who was giving one hundred and ten percent... By the end of September 1991, the *Slaves And Masters* trek stuttered to a halt with one-off shows in Poland, Athens and Israel. The feeling in the band was awful. No energy, no bright eyes, any future?"

Despite the fact that the sales of *Slaves And Masters* was underwhelming in comparison to Deep Purple's previous albums, the tour itself was arguably relatively successful. So much so that Turner was still a member of the band by the time it came to starting the writing and recording for their next album in 1992. However, with Deep Purple's twenty-fifth anniversary on the horizon and with pressures from management and indeed within the band itself, change was due to happen again.

Deep Purple - *Slaves And Masters*: In-depth

Chapter Four
The Legacy Lives On

Overall, *Slaves And Masters* received some good reviews in the music press but they weren't plentiful in number. Commercially, the focus was largely on younger groups and unfortunately for Deep Purple in 1990, they weren't one of them. An underrepresentation of the album in the music press can't have been good for sales. In an interview with Japanese radio in 1991, Ian Paice said, "Out of all the countries in the world, Britain is probably the hardest place for us to work. We still have a hard core of fans there but the musical direction in England is so far from what we do. We're stuck with all this dance and rap rubbish and that's what the kids are prepared to listen to. I love living in England, but as far as music is concerned it's a wasteland."

Slaves And Masters was reviewed in *Metal Hammer* in October 1990; "This band should call themselves Purple Rainbow, as *Slaves And Masters* sounds remarkably like any of the later Rainbow albums. The problem is that like Rainbow, it suffers from inconsistency with occasional flashes of inspiration dimmed by the dark recess of mediocrity. Opener 'King Of Dreams' demonstrates Purple Rainbow new boy Joe Lynn Turner's ability to twist a hook line into a silvered aural caress and is probably the most pleasing song on the entire album. He sounds huskier now than before and sounds, to his credit, better than ever. Other than that, there is little new or exciting to remark upon in a collection of songs which belong pretty much to twenty years ago. There aren't even any 'Knocking At

Deep Purple - *Slaves And Masters*: In-depth

Your Back Door's here from the 1984 reform album, *Perfect Strangers*. *Slaves And Masters* contains echoes of former glories though, the 'Lazy' reminiscent feel of 'Fire In The Basement' for one. The grandiose excess of early Purple are there in the form of the unnecessary and pompous string quartet opening to 'Love Conquers All'. You're better off buying *Deepest Purple* or 'Difficult To Cure'. Dull."

The album was reviewed in the *Gavin Report* in October 1990; "Deep Purple, here they are on only their fourth new label in over twenty years. Lately, the vocal slot has been the hot seat and it's recently been filled by the minstrel Joe Lynn Turner. Purple opens their album and phase four of their career with a mid tempo groove, 'King Of Dreams', already a solid album radio contender. This time around the band has found a good sounding halfway point between hard rock and radio friendly rock 'n' roll. The band has also stripped away a lot of the metal trappings, taking on a rehearsal room looseness, especially on tracks like the cookin' 'Highway Starish' (sic) 'The Cut Runs Deep' Ouch."

An interesting perspective there although admittedly, try as I might, I really can't see what 'The Cut Runs Deep' has about it that makes it reminiscent of 'Highway Star'. Am I missing something here? I don't think I am. In terms of musical characteristics and overall mood, the two songs are incredibly different. That said, they do both portray a band of virtuoso talents playing a song that is memorable. Of course, 'Highway Star' was so much more iconic than 'The Cut Runs Deep'; there's no getting away from that. Like many bands who were at their commercial peak in the seventies, it stands to reason that anything released thereafter was always going to be viewed as a point of comparison, even where specific musical similarities might not even be there!

Billboard reviewed the 'King Of Dreams' single in October 1990; "New line-up of (the) classic rock band resembles

Rainbow more than Deep Purple. But who cares? First shot from (the) *Slaves And Masters* album is a muscular, retro-vibed kicker that sounds great cranked up to ten while speeding down a highway."

Wow! The reason I say this is that upon reading some of the reviews relating to *Slaves And Masters*, it does make me wonder if the people doing them had actually listened to the music. They absolutely might have done. But is 'King Of Dreams' really a "speeding down the highway" kind of song? I ask this on the basis of, if the people reviewing *Slaves And Masters* didn't give it a listen, when it came to any reviews — good or bad — that the album got, it could have plausibly painted an inaccurate picture to those reading the review who may have been on the fence about whether to buy the album. I feel that this matters on the basis that Deep Purple were not at their commercial peak in 1990 but certainly, like any band, their work deserved a fair hearing prior to comment being made! A fairer assessment of the album would have probably been something along the lines of "It's not *Machine Head* but that's okay, because it's not trying to be."

Indeed, why should it matter that *Slaves And Masters* sounds more like a Rainbow album when there are so many positives about it overall? The album was reviewed in *Billboard* in October 1990; "Classic rockers return with a line-up that may remind some fans more of Rainbow than vintage DP. But personnel is secondary to the fact that this set glides back and fourth between seventies-vibed rock and nineties-styled metal with great ease. Tunes like bluesy 'Fire In The Basement' and fiery 'The Cut Runs Deep' showcase Joe Lynn Turner's fine, whiskey-soaked vocals and Ritchie Blackmore's restrained, but highly effective guitar work. A strong effort best enjoyed with the volume cranked up."

Fortunately, some reviewers gave credit where it was due, rather than bemoaning the fact that Deep Purple hadn't made a version of 'Highway Star' for the nineties. The 'King Of Dreams' single was reviewed in *Cash Box* in October 1990; "This single from *Slaves And Masters*, Deep Purple's first album in several years, is a melodic, mid-tempo item AOR programmers should check out. While 'King Of Dreams' isn't a blistering metal rocker a la 'Highway Star' or 'Smoke On The Water', the song has its share of muscle. 'King Of Dreams' was produced by Purple member Roger Glover."

With the power of hindsight, Jon Lord was keen to disregard *Slaves And Masters* as a Deep Purple album when he was quoted in *Keyboard* in January 1994; "The first reason that Deep Purple always made new starts is that we always said to ourselves: 'Let's prove ourselves to the people once again and make another really good album!' For example, with *The Battle Rages On...* we wanted to show that we can deliver better things than *Slaves And Masters*, which was really not a Deep Purple album at all. It carried the name, but the sleeve was deceiving."

The things people say retrospectively! From the same feature: "I myself was against Joe Lynn Turner from the beginning on. He just wasn't the singer I imagined. It's funny because in fact none of us wanted him, but he was the only one that was left. The guy we actually wanted, if we *had* to work with a replacement for Gillan, was the singer of Survivor (Jimi Jamison), a very nice, very quiet and very pleasant guy. He was an enormous Deep Purple fan and he would happily have taken over the job. But at the time he was afraid of his managers... They didn't want him to leave the band and he didn't dare to get into a fight with them. After a long period, during which we thought he'd accept the job, he turned it down. We were very disappointed and had to do auditions. There actually were a few good singers, but they were too young for us. I mean, Deep Purple isn't a young band anymore, but one with a long history and very complicated personal relationships. I think that every young musician would automatically be in a very weak position with us; he would be intimidated by the strong egos, who play a very big role for us. The feeling in the band would suffer from this shyness, especially on stage, where we really battle."

According to Turner though, in *Kerrang!* in March 1991; "Jon Lord's brother actually spoke to me when he heard *Slaves And Masters* and said that while he was always proud that his brother was in the band, he'd never really liked the music that much. It was too strange. Now he says he can dig it, which is cool."

In more recent years, *Slaves And Masters* has attracted a mixed range of reviews with some arguing that the album deviates too far from Deep Purple's signature sound and that Joe Lynn Turner wasn't right for the band due to being too close to the AOR style of rock that he made with Rainbow. Other fans are more open to the concept that *Slaves And Masters* is, despite being formulaic in places, an enjoyable album in its own right that offers a range of strong tracks. It is an album that some of MkV hold in high regard to this day.

In an interview with Joel Gausten in May 2016, Joe Lynn Turner said; "The strength of the songs and musicianship keeps it alive. It is the kind of record that stands the test of time very well."

Blackmore was quoted in *Fireworks* in 2013; "There was a period in the hard rock days when I was basically disgusted with whatever came out. That was nobody's fault but my own really. I was just playing, bored, it all sounded the same to me. No real excitement there, it was more like 'Thank God we've finished another one, just get it out.' Things like *Deep Purple In Rock*, *Machine Head*, *Burn*, they were great records, along with *Rainbow Rising* — they were all exciting. But some of the stuff in between, for me, was not anything to be really excited about. *Perfect Strangers* — I though that was a very good record. Then the second one (*The House Of Blue Light*),

I thought that was really bad. At the time, people thought we'd only stay together for one record. After that second one, maybe we should have called it a day, although, I really liked *Slaves And Masters* with Joe Lynn Turner. But again, I'm heavy into melody. A lot of people didn't like it simply because it was him, which I always found strange."

Slaves And Masters was plausibly a move forward for Deep Purple after *The House Of Blue Light*. After All, it kept four out of the five MkII line-up members working together whilst Turner occupied Gillan's seat for the duration of just one album. That's not in any way intended as a criticism to Joe Lynn Turner, far from it, but the fact is that after *The House Of Blue Light*, if Deep Purple disbanded entirely to the extent that they had all ended up going their separate ways, then would there have even been any more Deep Purple albums, ever? We'll never know but it's a consideration that adds weight to the idea that *Slaves And Masters* was an important part of Deep Purple's legacy, even if those who aren't keen on it are to consider it as a necessary bridge between *The House Of Blue Light* and *The Battle Rages On...*

Joe Lynn Turner said in March 1991; "Right now Ritchie's playing his ass off 'cause he's re-inspired. Let's face it, for better or for worse Purple wouldn't have been together if Gillan was still around... Take it from me, nobody in this band is a day at the beach! It's just that Ritchie's the best at it, and everybody else takes lessons from him!... Apparently it was obvious with Ian that he was creatively lacking, at least in a Purple direction. The way I heard it — and I got the inside shit — was that it was like that. *The House Of Blue Light* hurt more than anything else. People started to think that the band was going downhill. Let's face it, the credibility's been lost — or at least it's gone downhill — and we've got to fight like bitches to claw our way back up."

Upon being asked if the rest of the band saw it that way,

Turner replied; "In their minds, I don't think so. The rest of 'em have that 'Hey, we're Deep Purple' attitude. I think they're wrong. We have to work doubly hard because of the way the name's been tarnished. The signs are better than ever now. By the end of this tour we'll know each other that bit better, and we're already writing. If we're still together I think we'll come up with something brilliant. The signs for a new life are very hopeful and if there's enough support to warrant Deep Purple then it'll be great!"

Glover said in October 1990; "It was a very painful period leading up to the decision. I called him (Gillan) up afterwards to say we were still friends. The last Purple album we made, *The House Of Blue Light*, had been a very difficult one to make, not a happy one. The band didn't record it the way I wanted. I'm not the leader, but I am the producer and I had very strong ideas about the way we should have made the album and the band didn't want to do it that way. It turned out to be a stiff of an album and with a very wooden feel about it. So it was my idea to take a twenty four track with us, go on the road and record gigs for our live album. It didn't sell very well but it paved the way for this album (*Slaves And Masters*) which has been done much more like I wanted."

In Turner's view; "It sounds like Deep Purple but it's got a twist. We also believe in songs, and that's what sells a band. The guys felt they were severely lacking songs on *The House Of Blue Light* but they have them now."

Some saw *The Battle Rages On...* as an opportunity to get away from the musical stylings that had been predominant on *Slaves And Masters*. Jon Lord said in *Keyboard* in January 1994; "I had the feeling that we had to prove something with the new album (*The Battle Rages On...*). We had said to ourselves that when we were to record an album for our twenty fifth anniversary, it had to be a real Deep Purple album, not some surrogate Deep Purple album like *Slaves And Masters*."

Deep Purple - *Slaves And Masters*: In-depth

Disappointingly, when Deep Purple were inducted into the Rock And Roll Hall Of Fame, Turner wasn't included as a recipient of the award, something that did not go unnoticed by Blackmore, who, rightly so, publically addressed this. A message was issued on Blackmore's behalf on his official website; "Obviously, as you know from the post here, I have my reason for not attending the Rock And Roll Hall Of Fame ceremony, although I appreciate the award — however, I do think that they should have given an award to Joe Lynn Turner for when he was in Deep Purple — for his singing and writing on *Slaves And Masters* — a great record, one of my favourites."

Slaves And Masters is a treat of an album to listen to because the addition of Joe Lynn Turner brought out things in the other musicians that would have perhaps not have been possible with Gillan in the position of vocalist. For instance, would Gillan's vocal style have worked on tracks like 'The Cut Runs Deep', 'Wicked Ways' or even, 'King Of Dreams'? And of course, that's no criticism of Gillan; both he and Turner are excellent vocalists in their own right. Overall though, it's fantastic that via what Turner brought to the band, Deep Purple were able to go in a different direction; one that was interesting and one that showcased their talents in a different light through the exploration of going off-genre a bit from the MkII Purple sound. It is very much to Deep Purple's credit that they were never ones to sit back and be happy with doing the same thing over and over again (as a band or as individual musicians in their extra-curricular projects outside of Deep Purple). *Slaves And Masters* is a perfect example of that. Besides, *Slaves And Masters* sounds a lot more cohesive from one track to the next than *The House Of Blue Light*.

It is imperative not to overlook the specific amount of content that Turner brought to the table when he joined Deep Purple. In particular, he had initially recorded 'Too Much Is Not Enough' as an intended follow up to his first solo album, *Rescue*

You (1989). The song was also recorded by Paul Rodgers and Kenney Jones under the band name of, The Law. They didn't release it either though. In 1998, Turner recorded 'Too Much Is Not Enough' for his album, *Hurry Up And Wait*. Apart from 'King Of Dreams', 'The Cut Runs Deep' and 'Love Conquers All' (all of which have been performed by Turner on occasion as part of his solo performances), none of the material from *Slaves And Masters* has been performed live by Deep Purple since their 1991 tour. 'King Of Dreams' featured on the setlist for the Hughes Turner Project's European and Japanese tours in 2002. Their performance of the song features on their album released in the same year, *Live In Tokyo*.

In August 1992, having completed a world tour to promote his solo album, Gillan was on the cusp of launching a new band called Repo Depo. By some accounts, it was a close call but the offer to return to Deep Purple was just too good an opportunity to refuse. Colin Hart asserted; "Apparently, Ian had not had a good time of it away from Purple from a financial point of view, although his latest band Repo Depo was, in his estimation, the real deal and would make it. He told me much later that his decision to tour with Black Sabbath a decade before had been purely financial and he had never taken the trouble to learn the lyrics that he couldn't understand anyway... Once Ian agreed to return in principle, the band dispatched Roger to England with some of the tapes we had recently recorded with Joe for the new album, just to confirm that Ian could still hack it vocally. Nothing could be left to chance whatever the history."

Ian Gillan stated in his 1993 autobiography; "If I didn't much like the gigs, I did enjoy the social side of Sabbath, although we went from one crisis to another. We were arrested in Barcelona when I set fire to a waiter's jacket — apparently! Then all Sabbath broke loose with an amazing brawl on the street outside. When we had bailed out Geezer, Don (Arden) sent some people in from Germany to take care of us, and they were told to stay with the band everywhere after that. And, I mean everywhere. Don also deducted the cost of our appalling behaviour from the accounts."

Within a month of Gillan being back in the fold, the newly reformed MkII started work on a new album in 1992. Turner had already contributed towards some of the material that would come to feature on *The Battle Rages On...* In an interview for *Burrn* in October 1993 Blackmore was asked if the keys were changed for Gillan's voice; "I can't remember. I just know that most of the songs sound very different with Ian Gillan."

Joe Lynn Turner said to *Kerrang!* in March 1991; "It's a real feather in my cap (to be in Deep Purple) and I think that the album is a pretty good display of what I can do. But to be honest, in my opinion, the best of this album is still lying on the cutting floor. We've got some tracks that you'd fuckin' die for, but we never finished them. Ritchie wrote some riffs for a song called 'Just Don't Call It Love' that were fuckin' brilliant. One day I woke up and was told that we weren't doing them. I asked why, but with Purple you never get to know why. I hope we'll be able to make some use of them on the next album to establish a new, modern sound."

Damn! That's really poignant reading for anyone who likes the *Slaves And Masters* album; the things that could have been if this line-up of Deep Purple kept going! Of course, Gillan's return and *The Battle Rages On...* are both pivotal in Deep Purple's history as we know it and indeed, musically, something that many fans were glad to see happen. Equally though, it's fascinating to consider what a second album from the *Slaves And Masters* line-up could have sounded like and it's sad that we'll never know.

Turner's smooth melodic vocals were not only excellent on *Slaves And Masters* in and of themselves, but they also inspired the direction of the writing on that album; it would have been amazing to have a second album from that line-up of Deep

Purple because it could have served as a continuation of that style. After all, the opening track of *The Battle Rages On...* has "heavy riff MkII Deep Purple" written all over it. And that's not a bad thing — not at all! Far from it! I'm glad that album exists as much as anyone. But still, it speaks volumes about how different the *Slaves And Masters* album was in comparison to the output of MkII rounds two and three (so *Perfect Strangers, The House Of Blue Light* and *The Battle Rages On...*). It's a shame to think that *Slaves And Masters* was the only album recorded by MkV Deep Purple, especially in view of the fact that they were already working on a follow up together. The musical content on the album showed that the potential was certainly there. It was a strong writing team who weren't afraid to try something different.

Glover, Lord and Paice were cautious about doing another MkV album, as were Deep Purple's management. Commercially, the need to have Gillan back was not something that could be glossed over. Colin Hart recalled; "Bruce wanted to go back for Ian Gillan but was obviously finding Ritchie a tough one to convince. I don't think he had any argument with Roger, Paicey or Jon."

By spring 1992, there was still no official decision on who would be singing for Deep Purple. Nevertheless, Colin Hart was instructed to book Bearsville Studios in New York so that rehearsals and writing could begin for the next album. It was only part way through rehearsals that Turner was told that he was out of the band. According to Hart, Turner already had a sense that the band wanted Ian Gillan back. As Hart explained; "Ritchie stayed silent on the subject, Roger, as always, wanted to get on with the writing, staying away from any controversy. Hard call for him as he was one of Ian's best chums but had also served time in Rainbow with Joe very successfully — better to keep the old bandana head down. Bruce needed to bring in reinforcements to finally convince Ritchie that his nemesis Ian should be recalled — the record company. They, I believe, pointed out to him that *Slaves And Masters* had been a relative flop and if there was to be a renewed enthusiasm for the band from within BMG then it would be more forthcoming if Gillan was back in the "acceptable" line-up. Ritchie felt that some sort of blame was being placed at his door for the album's failure, never accepting that one of the prime reasons for Ian's departure in the first place, was himself. He reluctantly agreed and Bruce contacted Phil Banfield, who was still Ian's personal manager."

Jon Lord told *Keyboard* in January 1994; "I mean, Joe's vision on this band was not our vision. He wanted to make something out of the band, which it couldn't be and we wanted to change him into something, which he couldn't be. It was a marriage made in hell, not in heaven, and this hell became extremely hot very quickly."

It's difficult to gauge but it is plausible that Lord may have felt differently about the situation prior to going on tour with the *Slaves And Masters* album (unless of course, artists feel that they can't be candid on their feelings at the time due to the need to promote something positively). He said in December 1990; "I can't read the future but I certainly wish now we have a quiet time personnel-wise. I don't want to change anybody right now. And I wish that we retain the excitement because if we can't get excited we can't make our music more exciting. I like to feel that we still have a lot of music to contribute and can make good enjoyable albums that people want to hear and come to see us play, and I'm looking forward to that."

After leaving the band Joe Lynn Turner said he was very disappointed with the music Blackmore wrote for what would be *The Battle Rages On...* Blackmore responded to that in *Burrn* in October 1993; "He can say whatever he wants to. All I know is that he told me, that he liked the demos we did. I think he said that he would have done them differently than we did it with Gillan. He wanted to do it more in a pop style. I love pop music, and I still listen to ABBA, but Jon and Ian Paice are not into pop music. It was a weird situation with Joe. He really likes poppy, sentimental songs. So Ian Gillan recorded his vocals over the songs we originally did with Joe, and whereas Joe sang it more in a pop style, Gillan did it in a more aggressive way… Well, when people get kicked out of a group, they start spreading negative rumours and changing facts around. Joe was like 'I'm the only man for the job.' I can't help myself laughing. I've heard other people saying similar things after leaving a group. They start spreading wrong information, but the decision to lay Joe off was done by the whole band in the end. Joe didn't leave on his own. He should stop changing the facts around."

Naturally, Blackmore was reluctant to welcome Gillan back into the band. He was quoted in the same feature; "As soon as Joe was gone, everyone began to shout: 'So what now? Looking for another singer again?' In fact, that was my plan. But then Roger Glover said: 'We should get Ian Gillan back, what do you think?' And I said to him: 'I don't want some naked people in front of me again.' Of course Roger defended him by saying: 'That never happened!' I was just joking at the time, but Roger took it very seriously. He didn't get the joke. However — the relationship between myself and Ian Gillan might be very bad, but he is the singer for Deep Purple. When the reunion thing came up in 1984, I was offered to work with David Coverdale, but I refused. Without Ian Gillan, it would have been pointless. Of course, David and Joe are great vocalists. When I hear Gillan's voice on the radio, I always recognise him. And when I hear Joe, it's like 'Is that the singer of Survivor?' Of course, I love Joe. But he needs some rest now. Maybe it's because of his age, but something was wrong with his voice in the end."

Initially Blackmore wanted Mike DiMeo from Riot as the replacement vocalist; "I know him, because I've played football with him," Blackmore recalled, "and he's a very talented singer. But the other guys didn't want him in the band, so that didn't happen."

With Gillan back in Deep Purple, it is hardly surprising that Blackmore's time with the band wasn't looking like a sustainable prospect. There was little interaction between the pair as Blackmore explained; "We almost don't communicate. When we talk, it's just little things. When we sit down together at the table, Ian always sits far away from me. Our communication is very limited. It's like: 'Ian, how are you?' 'Thank you, all is well.' We are like two tigers in one cage. But we managed to do this record somehow. I think we both respect each other, but Ian is not interested in me as a person and vice-versa. But when we get on stage, everything changes. He knows how to make me laugh on stage, but overall, for me, Ian is a very boring person. I don't really know how to describe him. Perhaps he could be called a "rebel soul". We are both very quarrelsome since our school days. But he uses his aggressions in his lyrics and his singing. I'm a little bit different in that aspect. However, I will never forget this one joke he did on stage in Japan I think. He was introducing 'Perfect Strangers' and said: 'The next song is dedicated to the football team Perfect Street Rangers'… But the funniest thing happened afterwards. He said: 'That was a song called Perfect Street Rangers, and the next one is about…' We all thought: 'What is he talking about again now?' Every time we finished playing a song, Ian Paice and Jon had to explain what Ian was joking about, because Roger always took it a little bit too serious. We are united by one thing. We both hate the show business side. When journalists start treating Ian Gillan too seriously, he's always giving weird answers. He likes to give interviews in good company, because there are many journalists, who are just rude and asking corny stuff, so he just gives them "nonsense" answers, but with a serious face expression. I like that dry humour. Paicey, Roger and Jon are not into that. If you want to read the most boring interview, then read an interview with Roger Glover. Of course he likes to joke, too. But in a very strange way."

So there was certainly the use of humour to carry things through but that alone clearly wasn't enough. The tensions were high during the tour of *The Battle Rages On...* and it is well documented in the 2019 book, *A Nasty Piece Of Work* by Jerry Bloom.

Blackmore was pretty candid about the tensions surrounding *The Battle Rages On...* even before the problems reached a point that saw him leave the band; "At first that song was called 'Vicious Circle'. But then Ian finished the lyrics and called it 'The Battle Rages On...' I've found that it was a very strong name, and I said to Bruce, 'Let's call the album that, too.' Bruce started laughing and said that this name perfectly reflects the relationships within the group. I've used the riff for that song already a few years ago in Rainbow."

The Rainbow song in question is 'Fire Dance': "But it was much faster. I really like this riff and I played it to Jon, I think. And Jon said, 'That's a good riff, fits the song perfectly.' And then I told him that I've already used it in one of my earlier songs, but he said, 'There is nothing wrong about playing things you've written yourself.' And so the song was born. I think it worked very well within the context of the song. But I have to admit that I haven't heard the album. Well, maybe I should give it a listen... at some later stage, if I'm not busy looking out of the window and I'm in the right mood."

After calling it a day with Deep Purple, Blackmore made one more Rainbow album in 1995 — *Stranger In Us All* — with a whole new line-up including Doogie White on vocals. Thereafter, he turned his back on rock music to focus on his new project, Blackmore's Night. It wasn't until 2015 that he got a new line-up of Rainbow together with Ronnie Romero as vocalist for the purpose of touring.

Deep Purple - *Slaves And Masters*: In-depth

A re-mastered edition of *Slaves And Masters* was issued in 2012. It includes two bonus tracks. First of all, there is 'Slow Down Sister', which didn't make it onto the album the first time around. It is a clever track in terms of how the riff is reminiscent of the one used on MkIII's 'Stormbringer' — it breathes a whole new life into it but with a groove that makes it less heavy and more commercial (and who said that funky bass playing was only a Glenn Hughes thing?).

It also includes the single edit of 'Love Conquers All'. In 2013, another re-master was released and in addition to the latter, it included the single edit of 'King Of Dreams'. Notably, there are bootlegs in circulation that include an instrumental version of 'Slow Down Sister' from the studio sessions.

In an interview made for the behind the scenes video of 'Love Conquers All', Joe Lynn Turner said of MkV's first jam on 'Hey Joe'; "We recorded it on a sixteen track machine that Roger had set up and it came out brilliant, there's not one flaw in it. I mean, it's live and it's real, but it's not flawed and we're gonna put it out as a B-side some day."

The 2013 release of *Slaves And Masters* was reviewed in *Record Collector* in the October; "It's hard to name a major rock act from the seventies and eighties that didn't flirt at least occasionally with the big hair/synths/slick choruses AOR format. Here's Deep Purple's most extravagant piece of AOR-ness, originally released in 1990 as if all guitar music wasn't about to be completely retooled by grunge and alt-rock. Purple fans avoided *Slaves And Masters* in droves at the time, for several reasons. Firstly, and most importantly, the Purple MkII line-up's singer Ian Gillan was replaced here by Rainbow frontman Joe Lynn Turner, a talented singer but not the guy who most followers wanted to see up front. Secondly, the songs just weren't as good as anything from the MkII line-up's 1984 comeback album *Perfect Strangers*, or the album that followed it, *The House Of Blue Light*. Thirdly, *Slaves And Masters* was incredibly lightweight. Tracks such as 'Too Much Is Not Enough' were practically pop, a dismal concept for devotees of the band that had released *Fireball* and *In Rock*. Two decades later, the album doesn't sound quite as weak: the single 'Love Conquers All' is a highly listenable bit of melodic balladry, for example. Other tunes such as 'King Of Dreams' and 'Fire In The Basement' make at least a reasonable effort to match Purple's catalogue, though no one is likely to claim that these come close to Purple's best work. It's probably the cheesy eighties keyboard sounds that mess the songs up most. Still, it probably seemed like the right thing to do at the time."

For many, *Slaves And Masters* is not their favourite Deep Purple album, but it is nevertheless an often overlooked effort that is worthy of attention and appreciation. There is no denying the presence of talent, thought and skill that went into creating the album. It is an interesting phase in the careers of each musician that made up MkV Deep Purple and a relevant album for fans of any of the artists involved.

Slaves And Masters is a consistent, relevant and enjoyable album that offers lots of melodic interest from a group of seasoned professionals who played well together. Is it Deep Purple as many think it should be? Well, maybe not. Essentially though, it is very much a product of its time and certainly an important album — musically, commercially and as an interesting era in Deep Purple's legacy.

Deep Purple - *Slaves And Masters*: In-depth

Appendices

Personnel

Deep Purple
Joe Lynn Turner — lead vocals
Ritchie Blackmore — guitars
Jon Lord — organ, keyboards, string arrangements
Roger Glover — bass, additional keyboards, production, mixing
Ian Paice — drums

Additional Musicians
String orchestra led by Jesse Levy

Production Notes
Recorded in early/mid 1990 at Greg Rike Productions in Orlando, Florida
Additional recordings at Sountec Studios Inc. and the Powerstation in New York
Engineered by Nick Blagona
Additional mixing by Nick Blagona at The Powerstation
Raymond D'Addario — production assistant
Wally Walters, Peter Hodgson, Matthew Lamonica, Dan Gellert — assistant engineers
Mastered by Greg Calbi at Sterling Sound, New York

Cover Art
Painting — Thierry Thompson
Art enhancement — Ralph Werni
Art direction — Roger Glover
Photography — Dieter Zill

Track Listing

1. King Of Dreams (Ritchie Blackmore, Joe Lynn Turner, Roger Glover) — 5:26
2. The Cut Runs Deep (Blackmore, Turner, Glover, Jon Lord, Ian Paice) — 5:42
3. Fire In The Basement (Blackmore, Turner, Glover, Lord, Paice) — 4:43
4. Truth Hurts (Blackmore, Turner, Glover) — 5:14
5. Breakfast In Bed (Blackmore, Turner, Glover) — 5:17
6. Love Conquers All (Blackmore, Turner, Glover, Lord) — 3:47
7. Fortuneteller (Blackmore, Turner, Glover, Lord, Paice) — 5:49
8. Too Much Is Not Enough (Turner, Bob Held, Al Greenwood) — 4:17
9. Wicked Ways (Blackmore, Turner, Glover, Lord, Paice) — 6:33
(The vinyl edition has Fortuneteller as track 4)

2012 Friday Music re-mastered edition bonus tracks
10. Slow Down Sister (Blackmore, Turner, Glover, Lord, Paice) — 5:57
11. Love Conquers All (single edit) — 3:25

2013 Hear No Evil recordings re-mastered edition bonus tracks
10. Love Conquers All (single edit) — 3:25
11. King Of Dreams (single edit) — 4:51
12. Slow Down Sister — 5:57

Discography

UK
Original 5th October 1990 releases:
RCA PL 90535, LP
RCA PD 90535, CD
RCA PK 90 535, cassette

Reissues:
RCA 74321 18719 2, CD, 2012
Music On Vinyl MOVLP505, LP, 24th May 2012
Hear No Evil Recordings HNECD021, CD, 2013

USA
Original releases:
RCA 2421-1 R, LP, October 1990
RCA 2421-2-R, CD, October 1990
RCA 2421-4-R, cassette, October 1990

Reissues:
BMG Special Products 75517486982, CD, 2004
BMG Collectables COL-CD-8406, CD, 2004
Friday Music – 88765415342, LP, 2012

Japan
Original release:
RCA BVCP-25, CD, 21st October 1990

Reissues:
RCA BVCM-35012, CD, 25th March 1999
BVCM-35350, CD, 23rd July 2008
RCA BVCP 20003, CD, 9th December 2009
RCA SICP 30666, CD, 3rd September 2014
*All reissues except the 1999 version include the bonus track, 'Slow Down Sister'.

1991 Tour Dates

Sunday 4th February	Palac Kultury a Sportu, Ostrava, Czechoslovakia
Monday 5th February	Sportcsarnok, Budapest, Hungary
Tuesday 6th February	Dom Sportova, Zagreb, Croatia
Thursday 8th February	Halle Tony Garnier, Lyons, France
Friday 9th February	Palais Des Sports, Marseilles, France
Saturday 10th February	Palais Des Sports, Toulouse, France
Monday 12th February	Salle Galaxie, Metz-Amneville, France
Tuesday 13th February	Festhalle, Frankfurt, Germany
Wednesday 14th February	Eberthalle, Ludwigshaffen, Germany
Thursday 15th February	Olympiahalle, Munich, Germany
Saturday 17th February	Sporthalle, Hamburg, Germany
Sunday 18th February	Eissporthalle, Berlin, Germany
Tuesday 20th February	Grugahalle, Essen, Germany
Thursday 22nd February	Stadthalle, Freiburg, Germany
Friday 23rd February	Karl Diem Halle, Wurzburg, Germany
Saturday 24th February	Hallenstadion, Zurich, Switzerland
Monday 26th February	Palais Des Omnisports, Paris, France
Thursday 1st March	Globe Arena, Stockholm, Sweden
Friday 2nd March	Scandinavium, Gothenburg, Sweden
Sunday 4th March	Jäähalli, Helsinki, Finland
Monday 5th March	Forum, Copenhagen, Denmark
Wednesday 7th March	Ahoy Sportpalais, Rotterdam, Holland
Thursday 8th March	Forst National, Brussels, Belgium
Saturday 10th March	Labatts Apollo, Manchester, England
Sunday 11th March	Playhouse Theatre, Edinburgh, Scotland
Monday 12th March	NEC, Birmingham, England
Wednesday 14th March	Hammersmith Odeon, London, England
Thursday 15th March	Hammersmith Odeon, London, England
Friday 16th March	Hammersmith Odeon, London, England
Saturday 17th March	Hammersmith Odeon, London, England
Tuesday 10th April	Memorial Hall, Burlington, VT, USA
Thursday 12th April	Radio City, New York, NY, USA

EXPRESSEN ★ Lördagen den 2 mars 1991

Deep Purple sjunker allt djupare

KONSERT

DEEP PURPLE
Globen, Stockholm

I idrottsvärlden finns en skoningslös men väl fungerande automatik som årligen förpassar dåliga lag till lägre divisioner.

Ibland önskar man att det fanns ett liknande system i musikvärlden.

Deep Purple har inte skapat något vettigt sedan 1972 men lever ändå högt och stort på gamla meriter.

För Deep Purple är lika relevanta i 90-talet som IFK Holmsund vore i årets fotbollsallsvenska.

Lagkaptenen **Richie Blackmore** har ledsnat. Han har spelat samma låtar i 20 år. Han tycker inte att det är kul längre.

Och jag förstår honom.

Att spela riffet till "Smoke on the water", det första riff som varje festgitarrist lär sig, varje kväll i 20 år kan inte vara någon större kick.

Men det ursäktar inte att bandet gör en oinspirerad, urtrist rutinspelning för 4 000 personer som betalat över 200 kronor vardera för biljetterna.

Fredagen var ingen konsertdag för hårdrockens största och äldsta legendarer.

Det var bara ytterligare en dag på jobbet.

Fem i nio gick de på skiftet. Tjugo över tio stämplade de ut, klev in i duschen, kvitterade ut var sin väl tilltagen bunt tusenlappar och åkte hem till hotellet för att sova.

När pengarna inte bara blir en av drivkrafterna för ett rockband, utan den enda drivkraften är det dags att lägga av.

Och jag tror inte Deep Purple kommer tillbaka till Sverige någon mer gång. Jag tror inte att Deep Purple finns efter den här turnén.

I går visade den vanligtvis så entusiastiska hårdrockpubliken ovanligt tydligt sitt missnöje.

De klappade inte ens in bandet till ett extranummer.

Vilket Richie Blackmore förmodligen var glad för.

Då slapp han i alla fall spela "Smoke on the water".

— PETER ÖHMAN

Foto: JENS ASSUR

— SPELA LITE HÖGRE och snabbare, annars somnar jag. Varken Deep Purples nyinköpte sångare Joe Lynn Turner eller el maestro själv, Richie Blackmore, hade någon lysande kväll i Globen i går kväll. Efter en timme och tjugofem minuter på skiftet stämplade de ut och lämnade scenen utan ett enda extranummer.

Friday 13th April	Centrum, Worcester, MA, USA
Sunday 15th April	Joe Louis Arena, Detroit, MI, USA
Wednesday 18th April	The Bushnell, Hartford, CT, USA
Thursday 19th April	Tower Theatre, Philadelphia, PA, USA
Friday 20th April	Tower Theatre, Philadelphia, PA, USA
Sunday 22nd April	Syria Mosque, Pittsburgh, PA, USA
Saturday 12th May	Sports Arena, San Diego, California, USA *cancelled*
Tuesday 15th May	Desert Sky Pavilion, Phoenix, Arizona, USA
Wednesday 16th May	Pima County Fairgrounds, Tucson, Arizona, USA
Sunday 24th June	Budokan, Tokyo, Japan
Monday 25th June	Budokan, Tokyo, Japan
Tuesday 26th June	Castle Hall, Osaka, Japan
Wednesday 27th June	Budokan, Tokyo, Japan
Friday 29th June	Football Stadium, Bangkok, Thailand
Tuesday 3rd July	National Stadium, Singapore
Thursday 16th August	Ginasiodo Ibirapuera, Sao Paolo, Brazil
Friday 17th August	Ginasiodo Ibirapuera, Sao Paolo, Brazil
Saturday 18th August	Atuba Convention Centre, Curitiba,
Monday 20th August	Olympia, Sao Paolo, Brazil
Tuesday 21st August	Olympia, Sao Paolo, Brazil
Thursday 23rd August	Gigantinho, Porto Alegre, Brazil
Friday 24th August	Ginasiodo de Maracananzinho, Rio, Brazil
Friday 14th September	Football Stadion, Košice, Czechoslovakia
Saturday 15th September	Városi Stadion, Nyíregyháza, Hungary
Tuesday 18th September	Leisure Centre, Szombathely, Hungary
Sunday 23rd September	Hala Arena, Poznan, Poland
Wednesday 26th September	POA Stadium, Athens, Greece
Friday 28th September	Park HaYarkon, Tel Aviv, Israel

Broadcasted on Israeli Radio
Saturday 29th September	Tzemach on the Sea of Galilee, Israel

Velho Deep Purple. Salvo pelo rock.

As velhas bandas de rock — "dinossauros", como são chamadas — parecem estar destinadas a se tornar novas orquestras de Glenn Miller (ou de Ray Coniff, se preferir): todo ano elas voltam com novas formações e velhas canções para embalar os palcos periféricos do planeta.

São artistas que vivem do nome. Não, não se trata do brontossauro Bob Dylan, que cantou sexta e sábado na cidade, mas do Deep Purple, o grupo que teve seu tempo de glória metalóide no comecinho dos anos 70.

O Purple (que já tocou sexta e sábado no ginásio do Ibirapuera) se apresenta hoje a amanhã no Olympia, com um jovem cantor, um certo Joe Lynn Turner, que com alguns berros no estilo Bob Plant consegue assassinar os velhos clássicos da banda, enquanto Ritchie Blackmore, Roger Glover, Jon Lord e Ian Paice tentam recobrar o vigor de vinte anos passados, nem que para isso seja preciso usar roupas de couro justíssimas, ter ataques típicos de uma prima-dona e tocar a 9ª Sinfonia de Beethoven.

Lynn e Blackmore: um vale-tudo para manter viva a lenda.

O público quase lotou o Ginásio do Ibirapuera nas noites de sexta e sábado para cultuar seus ídolos quarentões. Formada por velhos hippies de cabelos grisalhos e jovens headbangers descabelados, a multidão aguentou firme um atraso de duas horas e meia na sexta, e de uma hora no sábado, para relembrar antigos sucessos como "Hush", "Child in Time", "Highway Star", "Lazy" e "Smoke on the Water", entre outros, e suportar algumas novas baladas heavy dignas das rádios FM. Mas a verdade é que esta gloriosa banda não tem mais o ímpeto de outrora, conseguindo mesmo atravessar o ritmo em algumas canções ("Lazy" foi lamentável). E, para piorar as coisas, Jon Lord ainda atacou de Chopin e Gershwin.

Mas não importa — afinal, mais uma "lenda viva" esteve aqui. E Ritchie Blackmore (que, dizem, é melhor jogador de futebol do que guitarrista) ainda quebrou sua guitarra no sábado, num sacrifício ritual há muito esquecido (o que me lembrou o filme **Top Secret — Superconfidencial**, quando Val Kilmer canta num restaurante e um músico bem velhinho despedaça sua guitarra contra o amplificador). O público gostou e aplaudiu. É só rock and roll. Quem não gosta?

Lu Gomes

Deep Purple no Olympia (rua Clélia, 1.517, tel.: 864-7333). Hoje e amanhã às 22h. Ingressos de Cr$ 9.000,00 a Cr$ 20.000,00.

In-depth Series

The In-depth series was launched in March 2021 with four titles. Each book takes an in-depth look at an album; the history behind it; the story about its creation; the songs, as well as detailed discographies listing release variations around the world. The series will tackle albums that are considered to be classics amongst the fan bases, as well as some albums deemed to be "difficult" or controversial; shining new light on them, following reappraisal by the authors.

Titles to date:
Jethro Tull - Thick As A Brick   978-1-912782-57-4
Tears For Fears - The Hurting   978-1-912782-58-1
Kate Bush - The Kick Inside   978-1-912782-59-8
Deep Purple - Stormbringer   978-1-912782-60-4
Emerson Lake & Palmer - Pictures At An Exhibition 978-1-912782-67-3
Korn - Follow The Leader   978-1-912782-68-0
Elvis Costello - This Year's Model   978-1-912782-69-7
Kate Bush - The Dreaming   978-1-912782-70-3
Jethro Tull - Minstrel In The Gallery   978-1-912782-81-9
Deep Purple - Fireball   978-1-912782-82-6
Deep Purple - Slaves And Masters   978-1-912782-83-3

Forthcoming:
Talking Heads - Remain In Light
Jethro Tull - Heavy Horses
Rainbow - Straight Between The Eyes
The Stranglers - La Folie
Alice Cooper - Love It To Death